Grammar Practice Activities

CAMBRIDGE HANDBOOKS FOR LANGUAGE TEACHERS

This is a series of practical guides for teachers of English and other languages. Illustrative examples are usually drawn from the field of English as a foreign or second language, but the ideas and techniques described can equally well be used in the teaching of any language.

In this series:

Drama Techniques in Language Learning – A resource book of communication activities for language teachers
by Alan Maley and Alan Duff

Games for Language Learning
by Andrew Wright, David Betteridge and Michael Buckby

Discussions that Work – Task-centred fluency practice *by Penny Ur*

Once Upon a Time – Using stories in the language classroom
by John Morgan and Mario Rinvolucri

Teaching Listening Comprehension *by Penny Ur*

Keep Talking – Communicative fluency activities for language teaching
by Friederike Klippel

Working with Words – A guide to teaching and learning vocabulary
by Ruth Gairns and Stuart Redman

Learner English – A teacher's guide to interference and other problems
edited by Michael Swan and Bernard Smith

Testing Spoken Language – A handbook of oral testing techniques
by Nic Underhill

Literature in the Language Classroom – A resource book of ideas and activities *by Joanne Collie and Stephen Slater*

Dictation – New methods, new possibilities
by Paul Davis and Mario Rinvolucri

Grammar Practice Activities – A practical guide for teachers *by Penny Ur*

Testing for Language Teachers *by Arthur Hughes*

The Inward Ear – Poetry in the language classroom
by Alan Maley and Alan Duff

Pictures for Language Learning *by Andrew Wright*

Five-Minute Activities - A resource book of short activities
by Penny Ur and Andrew Wright

The Standby Book – Activities for the language classroom
edited by Seth Lindstromberg

Grammar Practice Activities

A practical guide for teachers

Penny Ur

CAMBRIDGE
UNIVERSITY PRESS

PUBLISHED BY THE PRESS SYNDICATE OF THE UNIVERSITY OF CAMBRIDGE
The Pitt Building, Trumpington Street, Cambridge CB2 1RP, United Kingdom

CAMBRIDGE UNIVERSITY PRESS
The Edinburgh Building, Cambridge CB2 2RU, United Kingdom
40 West 20th Street, New York, NY 10011-4211, USA
10 Stamford Road, Oakleigh, Melbourne 3166, Australia

© Cambridge University Press 1988

First published 1988
Eleventh printing 1998

Printed in the United Kingdom at the University Press, Cambridge

Library of Congress catalogue card number: 87–27627

British Library cataloguing in publication data

Ur, Penny

Grammar practice activities: a practical
guide for teachers.
1. English language – Study and teaching
– Foreign speakers
I. Title
428.2   PE1128

ISBN 0 521 32944 2 hardback
ISBN 0 521 33847 6 paperback

Contents

Contents

Thanks

My thanks to Michael Swan for a number of good ideas; also to many colleagues, students and friends, who have both suggested new activities and provided practical, constructive criticisms of old ones.

Acknowledgements

The author and publishers are grateful to the following who have given permission for the use of copyright material.

The British Tourist Authority for the extracts on pp. 115–16, reproduced from 'Britain: A Land to Explore'; Britain on View Photographic Library for the photograph on p. 116; McGraw-Hill Book Company for the symbols on pp. 133–4 from *Symbol Sourcebook*, 1972, by Henry Dreyfuss.

Barnaby's Picture Library for the photographs by: Kirkby p. 65(1A), Howling p. 65(2B), Besley p. 66(3A), Coward p. 66(3B), Meadows p. 66(3C), Troisfontaines pp. 67(4A) and 142(3), Rodway p. 67(4B, 4C), Richter p. 109(6), Adlib pp. 241(1) and 242(5, 10), and Gibbs p. 252(4); Nigel Luckhurst for the photographs on pp. 65(1B, 2A), 107(3), 108(4, 5), 142(4), 241(3), 242(9) and 252(3, 6); Granada Television for the photograph on p. 106(1); Bill Godfrey for the photographs on pp. 107(2), 241(2, 4) and 242(6); John Walmsley for the photograph on p. 242(7); Jeremy Pembrey for the photograph on p. 252(5); and David Runnacles for the photographs on p. 252(1, 2).

The illustrations on pp. 56, 57, 86, 87, 88, 131, 169, 170, 182, 183, 184, 200 and 246 were drawn by Leslie Marshall; on pp. 117, 128, 166, 186, 199, and 201 by Chris Evans; p. 166 by Jenny Palmer; on pp. 167, 185, 210, 217, 219 and 220 by Clyde Pearson; on pp. 187, 217 and 218 by Shaun Williams; on p. 216 by Keith Howard; and on pp. 219 and 220 by Trevor Ridley

Book design by Peter Ducker MSTD

Introduction

I decided to write this book because I needed it; and as soon as I began to discuss the idea with other teachers and students it became clear that many of them felt the same need as I did, and for similar reasons. On the one hand, we all more or less took it for granted that we would have to teach grammar – either because some authority told us to, or because we ourselves were genuinely convinced that grammar input helps our students to learn the language. On the other hand, we felt most comfortable using a broadly communicative methodology in our teaching, and were disappointed to find that our coursebooks provided very few ideas for interesting, meaningful and contextualized grammar practice. There are usually either 'communicative' activities designed to develop general fluency, or 'grammatical' exercises that are for the most part based on uninteresting manipulation of forms. A few books and periodicals suggest a number of good ideas for the kind of activities we wanted (see BIBLIOGRAPHY) – but there seemed to be no comprehensive, systematically categorized collection that could be used to supplement a coursebook.

'What we need', a group of student teachers told me, 'is a book that will gather together the most useful of the game-like or communicative grammar-practice procedures that are in the books we know, plus any more you can think of or find, and lay them out systematically so that we can look up, say, the "Present Perfect" on Monday morning and find a few good ideas to choose from.'

I found, however, that however sensible and simple this idea sounded in theory, its execution in practice was not so easy; and the end result has inevitably fallen short of my first ambitious plans.

For a start the book could not possibly cover all the grammatical structures there are; nor is it always so clear what is 'grammar' and what is not. So I decided to select only those items that I and other teachers I consulted have found in our own teaching to be the most essential and/or tricky, and included some – 'numbers', for example – that are in the fuzzy area between lexis and grammar. Even then, the sheer number of activities which could be included in a collection of this kind is enormous, so it was necessary to sift and select. All this means that any individual reader will inevitably find some omissions.

Classification was another difficulty, as many of the best activities do

1

not divide neatly according to grammatical categories, but can be used equally well to practise several different ones. The final layout is inevitably a compromise solution, with a lot of repetition and cross-referencing, my main consideration being the convenience of the (teacher-)reader rather than consistency or economy.

Then there is the problem of acknowledgement. Many of the ideas presented in this book are borrowed, or adapted, from writers, teacher colleagues, contributors to EFL journals; and sometimes very nearly identical versions of the same activity can be traced back to two or more different sources. I have done my best to acknowledge sources wherever these are clear and known to me, and provided a bibliography; but there are doubtless omissions, for which I apologise in advance.

Acknowledgements for ideas are due to the following people in these activities:

1.2 Michael Carrier
4.2 Leo Jones
6.2 Mario Rinvolucri
11.2 Andrew Wright
12.6 Stretton Taborn
13.3 Michael Swan and Catherine Walter
15.2 Mario Rinvolucri
15.8 Michael Swan and Catherine Walter
17.3 Andrew Wright
17.4 Stretton Taborn
18.2 I.S.P. Nation
19.5 Mario Rinvolucri
23.9 Alan Maley
27.4 Alan Maley
27.5 Wendy Scott
28.5 Michael Swan and Catherine Walter
33.5 Michael Swan and Jennifer Seidl

PART ONE of the book – *Guidelines* – provides a general introduction to the topic of grammar practice, and suggests guidelines for the design of effective classroom activities; it also includes a section of practical hints to help you (the teacher) present them effectively in class.

PART TWO – *Activities* – consists of a series of descriptions of grammar-practice procedures, designed according to the principles outlined in PART ONE. The activities are grouped into sections according to grammatical category, and these ordered alphabetically; so you should be able to find any section you want simply by leafing through the book. If, however, you use different terminology from mine, look up your term in the index at the end of the book. Names of specific activities (*Association dominoes*, *Questionnaires*, etc.) are also included in the index. Where activities are mentioned elsewhere in the text, they are referred to by their section number and name, not by page number (4.1 *Association dominoes*, 15.4 *Questionnaires*).

The descriptions of the procedures are accompanied, where appropriate, by sample texts and visual materials in the *Boxes*, which you may want to photocopy for immediate use in the classroom (broken-line frames within the *Boxes* indicate cutting-out lines), or use as a basis for designing your own materials.

There is no formal classification of activities according to the mode (written or spoken) or difficulty level, partly because most of them can be used for both writing and speech, and at various levels of proficiency, and partly because you yourself are, obviously, a better judge of where and how to use them in your teaching situation than I am.

1 Grammar

1 What is grammar?

Grammar may be roughly defined as the way a language manipulates and combines words (or bits of words) in order to form longer units of meaning. For example, in English the present form of the verb **be** in the third person has two distinct forms, one (*is*) being used with a singular subject, and the other (*are*) with a plural; and if the plural *are* is combined with a singular subject, the result is usually unacceptable or 'ungrammatical'. Thus, a sentence like: *This is a book* is grammatical, whereas *This are a book* is not. There is a set of rules which govern how units of meaning may be constructed in any language: we may say that a learner who 'knows grammar' is one who has mastered and can apply these rules to express him or herself in what would be considered acceptable language forms.

I have not attempted here to describe the structures themselves, nor to define what is grammatically acceptable and what is not; for this you should refer to books of English grammar or usage (see BIBLIOGRAPHY). The function of this book is only to provide ideas for classroom practice.

2 The place of grammar in language teaching

There is no doubt that a knowledge – implicit or explicit – of grammatical rules is essential for the mastery of a language: you cannot use words unless you know how they should be put together. But there has been some discussion in recent years of the question: do we have to have 'grammar exercises'? Isn't it better for learners to absorb the rules intuitively through 'communicative' activities than to be taught through special exercises explicitly aimed at teaching grammar?

If you are (voluntarily!) reading this book, then your answer to the last question is probably either a straight 'no' or at least a cautious 'not necessarily'. The fact that a learning process is aiming for a certain target behaviour does not necessarily mean that the process itself should be composed entirely of imitations of that behaviour. In other words, ability to communicate effectively is probably not attained most quickly or efficiently through pure communication practice in the classroom – not, at least, within the framework of a formal course of study.

In 'natural learning' – such as the learning of a first language by a child – the amount of time and motivation devoted to learning is so great that there is no necessity for conscious planning of the learning process: sooner or later the material is absorbed. However, in a formal course of study, there is very much less time available, and often less motivation, which means that learning time has to be organized for optimum efficiency. This means preparing a programme of study – a syllabus – so that bits of the total corpus of knowledge are presented one after the other for gradual, systematic acquisition, rather than all at once. And it also means preparing an organized, balanced plan of classroom teaching/ learning procedures through which the learners will be enabled to spend some of their time concentrating on mastering one or more of the components of the target language on their way to acquiring it as a whole. These components may be things like spelling or pronunciation or vocabulary – or grammar.

Grammar, then, may furnish the basis for a set of classroom activities during which it becomes temporarily the main learning objective. But the key word here is **temporarily**. The learning of grammar should be seen in the long term as one of the **means** of acquiring a thorough mastery of the language as a whole, not as an end in itself. Thus, although at an early stage we may ask our students to learn a certain structure through exercises that concentrate on virtually meaningless manipulations of language, we should quickly progress to activities that use it meaning- fully. And even these activities will be superseded eventually by general fluency practice, where the emphasis is on successful communication, and any learning of grammar takes place only as incidental to this main objective.

3 What does learning grammar involve?

Before planning the organization of our teaching, we need to have clear in our minds exactly what our subject-matter is: What sorts of things are included under the heading *grammar*, and what is involved in 'knowing' a structure?

The sheer variety of all the different structures that may be labelled 'grammatical' is enormous. Some have exact parallels in the native language and are easily mastered; others have no such parallels but are fairly simple in themselves; while yet others are totally alien and very difficult to grasp. Some have fairly simple forms, but it may be difficult to learn where to use them and where not (the definite article, for example);

others have relatively easy meanings, but very varied or difficult forms (the past simple tense). Some involve single-word choices (*a/an/some*), others entire sentences (conditionals).

When we teach any one of these types of structures, we are – or should be – getting our students to learn quite a large number of different, though related, bits of knowledge and skills: how to recognize the examples of the structure when spoken, how to identify its written form, how to produce both its spoken and written form, how to understand its meaning in context, and produce meaningful sentences using it themselves. All these 'bits' may be presented in the form of a table thus:

ASPECTS OF THE TEACHING/LEARNING OF STRUCTURES

	Form	*Meaning*
Listening	Perception and recognition of the spoken form of the structure	Comprehension of what the spoken structure means in context
Speaking	Production of well-formed examples in speech	Use of the structure to convey meanings in speech
Reading	Perception and recognition of the written form	Comprehension of what the written structure means in context
Writing	Production of well-formed examples in writing	Use of the structure to convey meanings in writing

Some teachers, and/or the coursebooks they use, have a tendency to concentrate on some of these and neglect others: they may spend a lot of time on getting the forms right and neglect to give practice in using the structure to convey meanings: or they may focus on written exercises and fail to cover the oral aspects satisfactorily. It is important to keep a balance, taking into account, of course, the needs of the particular class being taught.

4 The organization of grammar teaching

Any generalization about the 'best' way to teach grammar – what kinds of teaching procedures should be used, and in what order – will have to take into account both the wide range of knowledge and skills that need to be taught, and the variety of different kinds of structures subsumed under the heading 'grammar'. Thus the organization suggested here represents only a general framework into which a very wide variety of teaching techniques will fit. I suggest four stages:

a) *Presentation*
b) *Isolation and explanation*
c) *Practice*
d) *Test*

a) PRESENTATION

We usually begin by presenting the class with a text in which the grammatical structure appears. The aim of the presentation is to get the learners to **perceive** the structure – its form and meaning – in both speech and writing and to **take it into short-term memory**. Often a story or short dialogue is used which appears in written form in the textbook and is also read aloud by the teacher and/or students. As a follow-up, students may be asked to read aloud, repeat, reproduce from memory, or copy out instances of the use of the structure within the text. Where the structure is a very simple, easily perceived one, the presentation 'text' may be no more than a sample sentence or two, which serves as a model for immediate practice.

b) ISOLATION AND EXPLANATION

At this stage we move away from the context, and focus, temporarily, on the grammatical items themselves: what they sound and look like, what they mean, how they function – in short, what rules govern them. The objective is that the learners should **understand** these various aspects of the structure. In some classes we may need to make extensive use of the students' native language to explain, translate, make generalizations and so on.

In more academic classes, or where the structure is particularly difficult for the students to grasp, this stage may take some time. However, where the structure is very simple, or very close to a parallel in the native language, or when the students tend to learn the language intuitively rather than intellectually, it may take only a minute or so or be entirely omitted.

c) PRACTICE

The practice stage consists of a series of exercises done both in the classroom and for home assignments, whose aim is to cause the learners to **absorb** the structure thoroughly; or, to put it another way, **to transfer what they know from short-term to long-term memory**. Obviously, not every grammar practice procedure can 'cover' all aspects of the structure as listed in the table on page 6; therefore we shall need to use a series of varied exercises which will complement each other and together provide thorough coverage.

With a structure whose formal rules are difficult to grasp, we might start by devoting some time to manipulation of the written and spoken forms, without relating particularly to meaning. Such practice is usually given through exercises based on 'discrete items' (a series of words, phrases or sentences with no particular connection between them, except insofar as they exemplify the structure to be practised). Commonly found exercises of this type are:

i) *Slot-fillers* (the learner inserts the appropriate item)
e.g. He is .... boy. We have .... umbrella. (a, an)
Answer: He is *a* boy. We have *an* umbrella.

ii) *Transformation* (the learner changes the structure in some prescribed manner)
e.g. This is a woman. (put into the plural)
Answer: *They are women.*

The function of such exercises is simply to help make the rules of form clearer and to ensure that they are learnt more thoroughly. A learner who has worked through a series of them may find it easier, eventually, to express him or herself correctly, in language that will be acceptable to a native speaker. But because they give no practice in making meanings with the structure (and are therefore, incidentally, usually not very interesting) these exercises have limited usefulness; so we should move on to meaning-based practice as soon as we feel our students have a fundamental grasp of the rules of form and their application. (They may, of course, grasp these rules adequately as a result of the presentation and explanation, in which case we will not need purely form-based exercises at all.)

Another category of practice procedures still stresses the production or perception of correct forms, but involves meanings as well – though as yet unlinked to any general situational framework – and cannot be done without comprehension. Such exercises are, again, usually based on discrete items, and tend not to be open-ended. Some examples:

i) *Translation*, to or from the native language

ii) *Slot-filling*, or *multiple-choice*, based on meaning,
e.g. He (works, is working, worked) at the moment.
Answer: He *is working* at the moment.

iii) *Slot-filling*, with choice of answers not provided,
e.g. Last night we .... television.
Answer: Last night we *watched* television.

iv) *Matching*

e.g.	He		an animal
	I	is	soldiers
	She	are	a woman
	The men	am	a student
	The dog		a soldier

Answers: *He is a soldier*, etc.

The language is still not being used to 'do' things, but merely to provide examples of itself (it is, in other words, not 'communicative') – but at least the exercises cannot be done through mere technical manipulation. They are certainly more interesting to do than purely form-based ones (and this interest can be increased by the introduction of piquant or amusing subject matter, or some game-like techniques), and provide more learning value.

The third, and probably most productive – certainly most interesting – type of exercise is that in which the stress is on the production or comprehension of *meanings* for some non-linguistic purpose, while keeping an eye, as it were, on the way the structures are being manipulated in the process. Such practice may be obtained through information- or opinion-gap communication techniques or through activities based on the production of entertaining ideas. For example, the students might discuss or write about the possibilities arising out of a dilemma situation using the modals *may, might, could, should*, etc. (see 17.8 *Dilemmas*), or make up stories to practise the past tense (23.11 *Cooperative story*).

If all three of the types of practice exercises described here are in fact used, they are likely to come in the order they have been laid out here – though not always. We may in the course of a communicative activity find that the students are making consistent mistakes in a certain structure and decide to return temporarily to an exercise that focuses on correct forms. Or it may be found feasible in some cases to do only one kind of practice (usually the third, as described above), if the structure is very easily mastered.

Most coursebooks and grammar practice books provide plenty of examples of the first and second types. This book, which is meant to act as a supplement to them, therefore concentrates – though not exclusively – on the third.

d) TEST

Learners do tests in order to demonstrate – to themselves and to the teacher – how well they have mastered the material they have been learning. The main objective of tests within a taught course is to **provide feedback**, without which neither teacher nor learner would be able to progress very far. We have to know where we are in order to know where to go next.

Formal examinations, usually preceded by revision on the part of the learners, and followed by written evaluation on the part of the teacher, are only one kind of testing, arguably the least useful for immediate teaching purposes. (I do not give here a list of techniques that can or should be used for formal grammar testing, since the subject is outside my terms of reference.) Most testing, however, is done automatically and almost unconsciously by teacher and learners as the course proceeds, the most valuable – though necessarily impressionistic – feedback on learning being supplied by the learners' current performance in class and in home assignments. Often 'practice' exercises are used to supply such informal feedback, in which case they may function virtually as tests: but if this aspect is stressed, their effectiveness as practice techniques is usually lessened (see the end of Chapter 2).

Of the four stages in grammar teaching described above, the *practice* stage is, I think, the most important, in that it is through practice that the material is most thoroughly and permanently learnt. So let us consider next what a grammar practice technique entails, and what makes it effective.

2 Practice

The practice stage comes after the initial presentation and explanation, when the learner is assumed to have perceived the material and taken it into short-term memory, but cannot be said to have really mastered it yet. Practice may be defined as any kind of engaging with the language on the part of the learner, usually under teacher supervision, whose primary objective is to consolidate learning. During practice the material is absorbed into long-term memory and the learner enabled to understand and produce examples of it with gradually lessening teacher support. A practice technique may involve reception – 'passive' exposure to spoken or written input – or 'active' production of language items and discourse.

What makes a language practice – or, more specifically, a grammar practice – procedure effective? There is, of course no one generalization that will answer this question, but some of the factors that definitely contribute to successful practice are the following.

1 Pre-learning

Practice is the second or third stage in the process of learning a structure (as described in the previous chapter) – not the first. The function of a practice procedure is to familiarize learners with the material, not to introduce it; learners should not be asked to practise material they have not yet been taught. This sounds obvious, but it is surprising how often teachers do in fact launch into practice activities in the classroom without sufficient initial presentation of the material. If effective pre-learning has not taken place prior to the practice – that is to say, if the material has not been clearly perceived and taken into short-term memory by the learners – then much time will be wasted on incomprehension or unacceptable responses, forcing the teacher to interrupt the procedure for explanations and corrections, and lessening the time available for real practice. If there is virtually unlimited time available, of course, as in a 'total immersion' situation, this does not matter so much; the learners will gradually understand and absorb the material through the practice itself. But such is not the case in most language courses.

There are apparent exceptions to the principle of pre-learning: when, for example, you introduce a structure for the first time in a brief sentence or two and then go straight into a perfectly well-functioning practice procedure. This happens where the structure's form and meaning are very straightforward, or consist of a simple variation of something already learnt, and the learners grasp it after being exposed to only one or two examples. Pre-learning has, however, still taken place, though using a rapid and almost casual presentation appropriate to the simplicity of the structure.

2 Volume and repetition

By 'volume' I mean the sheer amount of (comprehensible) language that is spoken, heard, read or written in the course of the activity. Crudely speaking, the more language the learners are exposed to or produce, the more they are likely to learn: this means devoting plenty of time to practice sessions, and exploiting that time efficiently. When the material to be practised is non-specific, as in fluency exercises, this just means spending as much time as possible **using** the language in general (as distinct from talking about it). When, however, the material is specific, as in the learning of a grammatical structure, most of the volume should consist of repetition of the items to be learnt. In other words, we want to design procedures that will induce the learners to engage with the items to be learnt as many times as possible. This does not mean mere mechanical reiteration of forms, but repeated reception and production, in speech and writing, of different examples of the structure's form and meaning.

In a brief exercise where there is insufficient volume and repetition, the learners may provide you with some feedback on what they know, or do not know, but they will not get much opportunity to consolidate their learning. In other words, the procedure will probably function as an informal test rather than as a practice.

In simple terms, the principle of repetition means that you have to get the learners to produce or perceive examples of the structure – say, sentences using the present perfect tense – over and over again. This would seem to be a perfect recipe for boredom. However, the two features of *interest* and *repetition*, though not easily combined, are by no means mutually exclusive; and thinking of ways to achieve both of them simultaneously is perhaps the central challenge facing the teacher and materials writer in designing effective practice techniques.

3 Success-orientation

Although it is certainly true that correction of mistakes does contribute towards learning (on a conscious, intellectual plane), the kind of thorough, semi-intuitive absorption of material we are aiming for in language teaching can only be achieved if, after mistakes have been eliminated, learners have plenty of experience of 'doing it right'. Thus practice in general is most effective if it is based on more or less successful performance, and practice activities should be designed and presented in such a way as to make it likely that learner responses will be acceptable.

Besides immediate efficiency of practice, this principle of success-orientation has wider pedagogical implications, no less important. A student whose performance is consistently successful will develop a positive self-image as a language learner, whereas one who frequently fails will be discouraged and demotivated. It should also be noted that tension and anxiety are fairly high if learners feel there is a possibility of 'failure' (that is, if they are in a sense of being tested), and are correspondingly lowered if they are confident of success. Thus, success-orientation contributes significantly to a positive classroom climate of relaxation, confidence and motivation.

On the other hand, the fact that there is no risk of failure in producing acceptable language lessens the challenge of the activity for some participants, so we have to find other ways of making it interesting (see Section 6 below, and Chapter 3).

4 Heterogeneity

A 'heterogeneous' exercise, as I am using the term here, is one which may be done at various different levels. Because most (all?) classes are in fact composed of mixed-ability groups, a 'homogeneous' exercise cannot possibly provide effective practice for all the students: it will be too difficult for the weaker ones, and/or lacking in volume and challenge for the stronger. It is, however, possible – and desirable – to design practice tasks that can be interpreted and performed at whatever level the individual student feels appropriate, so that some will be able to do more than others – in terms of both quality and quantity.

An example of an exercise lacking heterogeneity is one based on multiple-choice questions; for example:

A male chauvinist .... help with the washing-up.
a) don't
b) isn't
c) doesn't
d) aren't

Such an item can only be done by students above a certain level of proficiency, but on the other hand gives no opportunity for the really advanced ones to exercise their capabilities. An example of a heterogeneous task might be to give an initial sentence model, and ask students to contribute further examples. For instance:

A male chauvinist doesn't help with the washing-up. What else doesn't he do?

Students may respond with simple sentences like 'He doesn't cook', or more complicated ones like 'He doesn't approve of women going out to work.' In this way, the slower learners can succeed at the same time as the brighter ones can stretch themselves to the limits of their ability. Also, of course, the quicker ones can simply make **more** sentences, as well as more difficult ones, particularly if the exercise is done partly or wholly in writing.

An exercise which is not heterogeneous will provide you with more reliable feedback on learner performance, because the task is standardized and it is possible to assess the relative acceptability of different learner responses. But if this aspect is seen as a major objective, then the procedure is probably being used as an informal test, and is likely to be less effective as practice.

The use of heterogeneous exercises not only ensures that a higher proportion of the class get learning value out of the practice; it also, like success-orientation, has a positive effect on learner attitude and motivation. Response at many different levels can be 'right', hence these exercises provide an opportunity for the teacher to give slower or less confident students the approval and encouragement they need.

5 Teacher assistance

Having presented the practice task, we then need to make sure that our students do in fact perform it successfully, and fairly briskly (to get through as much volume of language as possible and to maintain interest). There should be very little correction of mistakes if there has been proper pre-learning, and if the exercise is really success-oriented. Teacher activity in the course of the practice should therefore be largely directed towards supporting and assisting the students in their production of acceptable responses rather than towards assessing and correcting. Examples of such assistance are: simply giving extra time to reread or think; repeating or simplifying a text; approving the beginning of an utterance in order to encourage production of the whole; suggestions, hints, prompts. All this means that we have to be very alert to sense when and where help is needed and what form it should take. Again, there is a wider 'message': I, the teacher, am here to help you, the learner, succeed and progress in your learning, not to judge, scold or make you feel inferior.

It may be argued that if we constantly help our students to get it right, we will never know if they can manage by themselves or not. Part of the answer to this is, of course, that we should be sensitive enough to feel when they are going to be able to produce acceptable utterances on their own, and not rush in to help unnecessarily. If, on the other hand, we let them get it wrong and then correct, there will have been virtually no practice: only a brief (failed) test, followed by a re-presentation of the correct form.

6 Interest

Interest in language-practice procedures may derive to some extent from extrinsic motivation: for instance, a student may be motivated to take part and succeed in exercises if by doing so he or she may earn class 'credit points' or 'stars', or if he or she badly needs to know the language for promotion at work. But such factors are based on success or failure in test-like procedures and therefore do not operate well in success-oriented practice; and they are often completely beyond our control and unpredictable (like how much the learner needs to know the language for career purposes). Thus, in most practice activities, motivation has to derive rather from the intrinsic interest of the activity itself: its (non-linguistic) topic and the task to be done.

An otherwise well-designed practice procedure may fail to produce successful learning simply because it is boring: interest is an essential feature of successful practice, not just an optional extra. Learners who are bored find it difficult to concentrate, their attention wanders, and they may spend much of the lesson time thinking of things other than the learning task in hand; even if they are apparently engaged with the exercise, the quality of the effort and attention given to learning drops appreciably. Moreover, because boredom, particularly in younger classes, often produces unruly behaviour, more valuable learning time may be wasted on coping with discipline problems. If, however, the class is interested in what it is doing, its members will not only learn more efficiently, they are also likely to enjoy the process and to want to continue.

For some practical ideas on increasing the interest of classroom activities, see pages 19–25.

Effective practice procedures, then, are usually characterized by the features of pre-learning, volume and repetition, success-orientation, heterogeneity, teacher assistance and interest. Any one particular exercise may of course lack one or more of these and still be effective in gaining specific objectives; but if too many of them are absent, the exercise is likely to become a virtual test, and provide little learning value.

For example, if you give five sentences with either *have* or *has* missing, and ask individual students to fill in the missing word, correcting them if they get it wrong – then this is what I would call a virtual test. There is relatively little volume or repetition, no particular success-orientation or teacher assistance, the exercise is homogeneous and lacking in interest. (The aspect of pre-teaching is difficult to illustrate in an isolated example.) You may find out which of the responders know the difference between *have* and *has* (hence the 'test' aspect), but will have done little to help those whose knowledge is still a little shaky and simply need practice. If, on the other hand, we tell the students about some interesting or unusual possessions of our own ('I *have*...'), invite and help them to describe some of their own to each other, and then challenge them to remember what possessions another student *has* – there will be volume, repetition, etc., and the exercise is likely to produce effective practice (11.4 *Possessions*).

Unfortunately, 'virtual test' procedures are extremely common in the classroom – being much more convenient to design and administer than real practice ones – and teachers and coursebook authors are often unaware that they are testing more than teaching.

So far we have looked at topics connected with the place of *grammar* in language teaching and how it may, or should, be taught; and we have considered some aspects of language *practice*, within the context of grammar teaching. It now remains to turn to the third word in the title of this book and see how some of the theoretical ideas dealt with up to now can be applied in the design and presentation of classroom *activities*.

3 Activities

This book does not set out to provide a comprehensive taxonomy of all the types of grammar exercises available to the teacher, but rather to suggest a number of interesting, game-like or communicative practice techniques that can be used to supplement those provided by regular coursebooks. In this chapter, we move on to a discussion of topics to do with the practical design of such techniques: the structure of the *task* on which they may be based; factors that contribute to *interest*; various useful models of learner *activation*.

1 The task

The task the learners are asked to do may be overtly language-based ('Give me some examples of "yes/no" questions') or apparently non-linguistic, producing use of the structure as a natural by-product ('Guess what I'm thinking of'). The function of the task is simply to activate the learners in such a way as to get them to engage with the material to be practised. 'Activating' the learners, incidentally, or the phrase 'active language use', usually means actual production of instances of the structure on the part of the learners themselves – but not always: in many cases learners are rather perceiving, discriminating, understanding or interpreting – processes which also involve a high degree of mental 'activity'.

The two essential characteristics of a good language-practice task are: a *clear objective* accompanied by the necessity for *active language use*.

a) CLEAR OBJECTIVE

The task objective may be language-based, in which case it may be generally defined as 'getting the language right'. However, the objective 'getting the language right' on its own often leads to the composition of rather boring, meaningless language-manipulation tasks, such as putting a series of sentences into the past tense.

If the main objective, however, is to get some non-linguistic result the task is usually much more interesting and has more learning value – provided, of course, that achieving the objective involves using the grammar. This objective may be, for example, to solve a problem, to get

17

someone to do something, to create some kind of pleasing composition, to explore a situation, to get to know one another.

In the most successful grammar exercises, the two kinds of objectives are combined, the non-linguistic one being the main motivating focus, while both teacher and students are aware of the 'secondary', linguistic one. You may say, for example: 'I want you to guess what I'm thinking of – and use "yes/no" questions as you do so.' The amount of attention paid to each aspect varies: if students get involved in discussing personal feelings while describing past experiences, it obviously will be inappropriate to ask them to concentrate on using the past tense correctly; but if the objective is to produce or edit something for publication, correct usage will be stressed.

In any case, the objective should be a simple one that can be defined in a few words, so that students are clear in their minds at all stages where they are going, and what the point is of what they are doing. It is very much easier to define an objective if there is a tangible result to be achieved: a list to be written out, a solution to be found and displayed, a story to be narrated, a picture to be drawn or marked. In such cases, you can explain the non-linguistic objective in terms of the end product ('Find and write down the solution to this puzzle . . .') rather than in terms of the process ('Suggest some ways you might solve this . . .').

b) ACTIVE LANGUAGE USE

The learners should be able to attain the objective only by an exertion of effort in some kind of active language use; though this, as noted above, may involve the so-called 'passive' skills, listening and reading. And this active language use should provide for repeated exposure to or production of the structure(s) being practised. In other words, our task must provide for **volume** and **repetition**.

First, we should make sure that the activity is in fact based mainly on using language and and does not waste too much time on mime, artistic creation or silent brain-racking. This may sound obvious, but it is surprising how many otherwise excellent language-practice tasks fall into this trap. It is tempting to think that if students (particularly children) are happily absorbed in doing a task in an English lesson, they are therefore learning English – but it is not always so. They may, of course, be achieving other equally – or more – important educational objectives, for the sake of which we may opt, temporarily, to sacrifice language-learning efficiency. But in any case, we need to be aware of what is really going on: to keep a careful eye on how much they are actually engaging with the language they are supposed to be practising.

Second, we may need to put certain constraints on the process of achieving our task objective in order to make sure that maximum language use in fact takes place. For example, if you ask students to fill in information (using the past tense) on an empty grid by referring to another, completed, grid, then they will simply copy out each bit of text into the appropriate square. If, however, you put them in pairs, where one student has one partially-filled grid and his or her partner the other, and they have to ask and answer in order to get the information, the amount of language used will be much more, and will include oral work and both interrogative and affirmative forms (see 23.8 *What really happened?*).

If we design our task in such a way that it has clear linguistic and non-linguistic objectives and obliges learners to engage repeatedly with the structure that is being learnt in the process of achieving them, then we have the basis for a good grammar practice activity. But it is only the basis. Learners may still not do it very well if they find it boring.

2 Interest

Learners may, as already noted, be motivated to participate in a learning exercise by extrinsic factors that have nothing to do with the nature of the activity itself – they may very much need to know the language, for example, or want to be approved of. But we are concerned here with intrinsic motivation: what kinds of features within the activity itself arouse learners' interest and attention and make them want to take part in it?

a) TOPIC

The (non-linguistic) content of the activity is obviously a major factor in arousing – or deadening! – learner interest. The importance of the topic as a focus varies: if the activity is a discussion or essay on a controversial subject, then obviously the topic must be one that holds the learners' attention; but if the activity is a game-like one where the emphasis is on problem-solving or creating amusing juxtapositions – as in an exercise like 17.3 *Desert island equipment* – then the subject matter becomes relatively unimportant, and the task itself is what provides the interest.

There is no single 'recipe' for the selection of subjects that will arouse learner interest, but it may help to ask yourself the following questions: Is my topic something my students can relate to because they know something about it and it arouses definite positive or negative reactions? Or alternatively, something they would like to find out more about, and can do so through participating in the task? Is it something which stimulates their imagination or curiosity? Or something they are already familiar or personally involved with and would like to discuss or tell others about? Is it something I am interested in and can communicate my enthusiasm about to the class?

If the chosen topic gives a positive answer to one or more of these questions, it will probably be found interesting ... but then again, it may not: even experienced teachers find themselves constantly surprised by the unpredictable reactions of their students to topics they had thought would interest or bore them.

A more reliable piece of advice is: **vary**! A common reason for the dryness of many language textbooks is the lack of variety of their subject matter. They tend to concentrate only on anecdote, or only on the domestic doings of a set of characters, or only on informational newspaper articles, for example, and fail to cover a sufficiently wide range of subject matter. The same is true of teachers: many of us get into the rut of certain types of subjects, and neglect to change them. Not only does a frequent change of topic in itself help to maintain attention and interest in the classroom, it also makes it more likely that sooner or later every student may get to something that interests him or her.

A good range of subject matter on which to base grammar practice might include the following types:
– Factual information on topics of general interest: history, geography, psychology, politics, science, etc.
– Controversial subjects of local or general interest
– Personal viewpoints, experiences, feelings, tastes
– Fiction: novels, short stories, anecdotes, folk tales
– Amusing or pleasing ideas as expressed in poetry, proverbs, quotations
– Entertainment: films, plays, television programmes
– Personalities: locally known people, famous celebrities, imaginary characters

b) VISUAL FOCUS

It is very much easier to concentrate on thinking about something if you can see that something, or at least see some depicted or symbolic representation of it. Learners (particularly, but not only, younger ones) who are asked to discuss or listen to something without any visual focus often find their attention wandering. This is because sight is an extremely powerful and demanding sense: if you do not provide your students with something to look at, they will seek and find it elsewhere, in objects that have nothing to do with the learning task and that may distract them. An exercise that uses both aural and visual cues is likely, therefore, to be more interesting than one that is only speech-based.

A written text may provide sufficient visual focus in itself; but accompanying graphic material often improves comprehension and performance if it helps to elucidate difficult content, adds meaning to a very short or boring text, or is used to compare and contrast ('The text says she's dancing but in the picture she's sitting down'). Such material is usually in the form of a picture – a poster, a magazine cut-out, a slide or overhead transparency – but it may of course be a representation of the information being talked about in brief notes or a diagram. You yourself are often an excellent visual aid, when using your own facial expression and physical movement to illustrate a topic; so are your students and the classroom environment.

c) OPEN-ENDEDNESS

A task that is open-ended allows for lots of different learner responses during its performance, and is therefore conducive to the production of varied and original ideas.

Even if the basic structural framework of the response is prescribed in advance, learners' motivation to participate rises significantly if they are allowed to choose the actual 'content' words to use: the contributions, written or spoken, become less predictable and more interesting. For example, supposing you want to practise adverbs of frequency: one technique is to supply a sentence such as *He has coffee for breakfast*, and then ask students to insert the adverb *always*. The result is boring because it is predictable and of totally uninteresting content. But if students are asked to suggest all sorts of things they *always* (or *usually*, or *sometimes*, etc.) do when, say, they are feeling depressed, or when they have a free day, the exercise immediately becomes more interesting for all participants (2.4 *What do you do when...?*). True, it also means they have to find their own vocabulary: but usually they can manage with what they know; and you can always supply the occasional new word as needed.

However, it is not true to say that all closed-ended tasks are boring. When you want to drill certain patterns that the learners still have difficulty in producing on their own, there is a place for activities based on very controlled responses; and these can be made more interesting by varying intonation, facial expression and gesture, by the use of visuals, or by introducing game-like features such as competition, time limits, role-play and so on (see, for example, 11.3 *Detectives*).

d) INFORMATION GAPS

The existence of information gaps should not be taken to be the sole criterion of genuine 'communication': there are many examples of language use that is obviously communicative in spite of their absence (greetings, for example, or joking repartee). But it is true that the transmission of new ideas from one participant to another does occur in most real-life language-based transactions; and when this factor is built into a classroom language learning task, the effect is to add a feeling of purpose, challenge and authenticity which improve learner interest.

For example, learners are often asked to practise the interrogative by taking an answer and reconstructing the question; a useful exercise for

sharpening awareness of interrogative forms, but certainly not outstand-
ingly interesting. If, however, students interrogate each other in order to
get the necessary information to fill out a form (15.8 *Filling in forms*),
then they are asking questions whose answers they do **not** know in
advance, but need in order to perform a task; and their interest in both
question and answer is likely to be much greater.

A variation of the 'information gap' is the 'opinion gap', where the
communication involves a transfer of ideas or opinions rather than facts.
The interest generated by opinion-gap activities is similar to that of
information-gap ones, but with the added feature of 'personalization'.

e) PERSONALIZATION

By *personalization* I mean the use of interaction based on the students'
personal experiences, opinions, ideas and feelings.

Too many textbooks seem to see the learners merely as potential
containers of knowledge, and neglect to relate to them as individual
people. This expresses itself in exercises which ask them only to do things
such as to express objective facts, or to manipulate texts about unknown
characters, or to discuss issues that do not touch their (the students') own
lives, and in a lack of tasks demanding any kind of subjective judgement
or individual variation. From an educational and moral point of view, I
find these kinds of books uncongenial; it seems to me a basic tenet of
good teaching that the teacher-student relationship should be built on the
entire personalities of both teacher and student, like any other human
relationship, not just on their language-teaching or language-learning
faculties. But also from the point of view of interest, to fail to relate to the
students' individual backgrounds, thoughts and feelings is to deprive
ourselves of an excellent source of interesting activities.

As an example of a non-personalized exercise, learners can be asked to
practise present perfect forms by discussing how long something shown
in a picture *has gone on*, or *has been going on*. This can be a useful,
heterogeneous exercise providing plenty of use of the structure. But a
much higher level of interest is likely to result if we ask students to talk
about things they themselves *have done* or *have been doing* (as in 26.8 *I
have lived here for...*). Their contributions are interesting not only
because they are unpredictable and likely to be very varied and original,
but also because there is an element of personal investment: the students
are 'giving' of themselves to each other. This not only raises the level of
attention to what is said, it also tends to contribute to an atmosphere of
warmth and friendliness within the class.

A word of caution, however: asking students to be very intimate or
frank with one another can sometimes cause embarrassment or even
distress; we have to be sensitive to their personalities and relationships,

and not ask them to 'give of themselves' more than they feel comfortable doing.

f) PLEASURABLE TENSION

The reason why most games are interesting is that they provide their participants – and sometimes spectators – with a feeling of pleasurable tension; and this feature can contribute also to the interest of language-practice activities.

The introduction of pleasurable tension, however, does not necessarily mean that the activity may be called a 'game'. There is a fundamental difference between a true 'game', played for fun and recreation, and a 'game-like' language practice procedure which is a serious goal-oriented activity, performed primarily for the sake of its contribution to learning. The distinction is, it is true, largely one of pedagogical approach and presentation rather than of practical design; but it is, I feel, an educationally valid and significant one.

A grammar practice activity, then, should be presented to the class frankly as such, but may be made more enjoyable and interesting to do by the introduction of an element of tension associated with game-playing. Such tension is enjoyable because it is rooted in the drive to achieve some stimulating and clearly-defined objective, with the spice of uncertainty as to results, but without any threatening real-life consequences attending failure.

For example, if the class is shown a picture and invited to make up sentences about it using the present progressive, the objective is rather ill-defined, and there is no particular challenge involved. If, however, we rephrase the objective: 'Make up 20 sentences about a picture using the present progressive', there is an immediate rise in tension (can we get to 20 or can't we?), and interest increases. We can increase it still further by introducing a time limit ('Make up 20 sentences about the picture using the present progressive within two minutes') and/or an element of competition ('Which group can make the most sentences about the picture using the present progressive in two minutes?'). I have tried out this sequence of exercises several times, and in every case the motivation to participate – and the amount of language produced – increased with each step (see 16.1 and 16.2 *Describing pictures*).

The factors which produce this kind of pleasurable tension as illustrated in the above examples are: the motivation to perform a clearly-defined, attainable but not too easy task; the added challenge caused by the introduction of extra constraints and rules, such as a time limit; the drive to compete with others (or with oneself, as in activities based on breaking one's own previous record).

One other useful generator of tension is the unexpected: what is going to happen next, and will we/they be able to cope with it? For example, in activities like 23.10 *Alibi*, or 15.9 *Don't say yes or no*, the tension depends on the unpredictability of the questions that will be fired at the answerers, and on their ability to think up acceptable answers.

g) ENTERTAINMENT

Another source of interest is sheer entertainment: the reception or creation of ideas or graphic forms that are in some way aesthetically pleasing or amusing, or both. Listening to stories or songs or watching films or plays or television programmes can obviously give pleasure; perhaps more effective for our purposes are those activities where the entertainment is supplied by the students' own contributions.

Exercises that are based on combining or comparing ideas not usually juxtaposed can produce all sorts of amusing results: 17.3 *Desert island equipment*, for example, where participants have to find reasons to justify using unexpected and incongruous articles on a desert island. Apparently straightforward brainstorming procedures often produce entertaining contributions: how many things can you think of that you might/could do with a pen, for example (17.2 *Uses of an object*): students get pleasure from both composing and hearing (or reading) original ideas. More serious, but equally pleasing, results can be obtained from activities like 3.2 *Cooperative poem*, where students contribute ideas connected to a central theme, and these are all put together to form a free-verse composition.

Sometimes providing entertainment can become the main objective of student contributions to a task, instead of a pleasing by-product. In a variation on 17.4 *Modal symbols*, for example, students compete to see who can suggest the most original or amusing interpretation of an obscure symbol.

h) PLAY-ACTING

Learners often enjoy 'being' someone else, or being themselves in an imaginary situation. And a temporary departure from reality, incidentally, is not only a means of motivating learners to participate, it is also a very effective way of widening the range of language available for use: if the students are acting the roles of explorers in the jungle, or soldiers in an army, or young children arguing with adults, they will be able to use varieties of language not usually appropriate for learners in the classroom.

There is a difference between *role-play*, where each student takes on a particular personality for an individual purpose, and *simulation*, where the entire group is talking through an imaginary situation as a social unit – though the two may, of course, be combined. Either may provide a framework for some excellent grammar practice, both controlled (see

15.1 *Dialogues*) and relatively free (20.6 *Election campaign*). Many information-gap and opinion-gap activities can function far more interestingly and effectively if given the added dimension of a simulated non-classroom situation. For example, exchanges based on giving and taking can be given the imaginary context of shopping (8.5 *Shopping*); or problem-solving can be made more immediate if the participants role-play the people involved (17.8 *Dilemmas*).

3 Learner activation

A well-designed grammar practice activity, then, should be based on a task that has clear objectives and entails active use of the structure being practised; and it should maintain learner interest and motivation through careful choice of topic, use of information-gap procedures, role-play, personalization, etc.

But much of the effect of all this may be lost on a large proportion of the class if we do not do something to ensure maximum, balanced participation of its members. When the activity is based on writing or silent reading, or on listening by all the class to a central source of spoken text, then participation is less of a problem: all the students are, potentially, equally activated. The problem arises when we want them to **speak** – and this happens in most classroom exercises. How do we activate learners in such a way that as many of them as possible participate in oral work?

The way learners are activated when performing an exercise, moreover, may affect not only the amount of participation, but also the level of motivation and involvement, and the learning value of the practice given; and here we are talking about reading, writing and listening as well as speaking. Some modes of activation are more appropriate and efficient than others for certain types or stages of practice.

In this section I shall describe the main techniques of learner activation available to the teacher – some of which are rarely if ever used in many classrooms – and try to assess the advantages and disadvantages of each for various teaching situations or kinds of practice activities. The techniques are set out more or less in the order in which they are likely to be used in teaching. In the first two, which are based on language reception with little or no learner response, it is the teacher who does most, if not all, of the language production, and clearly controls what little learner activity there is. In one-to-one teacher-student exchanges – probably the most common form of classroom activation – the teacher is still dominant, but there is increasingly active participation on the part of the learners. This participation increases still further in brainstorming or 'chain' techniques; and in most forms of pair or group work, nearly all the actual language production is in the hands of the learners, the teacher merely providing instructions and materials and acting as monitor and helper.

a) RECEPTION WITH NO OVERT RESPONSE

Initial presentation of grammar is often done through showing learners the structures within a written or spoken context, without demanding from them any immediate response beyond general comprehension. This technique can be used also to provide some very useful practice at the early stages. Listening to or reading large amounts of 'comprehensible input' is a far from passive process and arguably one of the best ways of familiarizing learners with acceptable forms – certainly one of the most natural and simple. Its use is most effective in situations where the learners are young, or learn better through intuition than through intellect, and where there is plenty of time available – as in a 'total immersion' type of course.

Texts used for simple exposure in this way should be selected or composed to present instances of the grammatical structure being learnt in as natural a context as possible: an advertisement, for example, is likely to produce instances of comparative and superlative adjectives. Such texts can later serve as models for compositions, or bases for interactive tasks.

However, silent listening or reading by students can be boring, especially if the topic is uninteresting; and it provides no opportunity for the teacher to monitor their learning: are they in fact engaging with the language or not? Sometimes you can tell simply through 'body language'; but it is easier if they have to give some overt response.

b) RECEPTION WITH MINIMAL RESPONSE

As well as giving the teacher an opportunity to monitor their learning, the necessity to make responses helps learners to concentrate on the exercise as a whole, and focuses their attention on the particular points being taught.

In minimal-response activations the learners are given a written or spoken text – which may be an isolated sentence or a longer passage of discourse – and asked to react to some aspect of it by physical gesture, brief answers, or written symbol. Discrimination exercises, for example, where the learner picks out examples of specific items (5.1 *Looking at advertisements*) come under this category, as do those requiring brief physical or verbal responses to questions (11.1 *Bingo*, 12.1 *Simon says*).

But of course there is still no production by learners of the grammatical structure in full-sentence contexts.

c) TEACHER-STUDENT EXCHANGES

The most common kind of verbal interaction in the classroom is the teacher-student 'ping-pong' exchange: the teacher asks a question or elicits responses in some other way, a student responds, the teacher approves or corrects and asks again, another student responds, and so on. The choral response – where two or more students answer together – is a variation of this, as are the 'performances', where students recite longer given texts or dialogues in response to teacher requests. Essentially, the teacher is the focus of attention, and is in full control of learner responses, largely able to determine what these will be, and in a position to monitor them.

This technique is most convenient to use at an early stage in practice when you wish to make sure that the learners are hearing and producing acceptable forms; but it has disadvantages. There is usually (except in the case of extended 'performances') a high proportion of teacher talk, hence relatively little language production by the learners; and the cues, since each demands only one response, tend to be geared to a single level, thus not providing very useful practice for very slow or very advanced members of the class. Since each exchange is 'closed' to participation by other members of the class, they often do not bother to listen to each other's responses and another potential source of learning is lost.

The parallel in writing is the textbook exercise where the learner writes the answers to a series of questions or cues. Here, of course, there is no problem of activating only one student at a time, and these exercises, given as homework, can provide a useful controlled follow-up to a classroom exercise.

d) STUDENT-TEACHER EXCHANGES

There is also the possibility of a reverse 'ping-pong', where the student initiates the exchange, and the teacher responds. This is a useful technique which is rarely used – perhaps because teachers do not like to forgo the initiative! Its advantage is that while the teacher can still monitor learners' utterances and provide good models of acceptable grammar, the learners themselves can decide on the content, and initiate their own ideas. Because of the originality of their contributions, students tend to listen to each other much more than in the conventional 'ping-pong' described above. This technique is particularly good for practising interrogative forms (15.10 *Preparing interviews*).

e) BRAINSTORM

In a brainstorm, the students are given a single stimulus which serves as the cue for a large number of responses. The stimulus may be a question with plenty of possible answers (2.4 *What do you do when...?*); or a picture to be described, commented on or asked about (16.1 *Describing pictures*); or a phrase or brief text that can be expanded in different ways (6.2 *Finishing conditional sentences*); or a problem demanding diverse solutions (17.8 *Dilemmas*).

The advantages of this technique are that it provides a larger volume of productive language practice on the part of the learners relative to the contribution of the teacher, and that it allows students to compose utterances at levels convenient to them. It also encourages originality and humour, and many brainstorming activities produce interesting and amusing results. The wide range of possibilities open to the participants and the fact that many of them are original and entertaining means that students tend to be motivated to contribute and the activity usually moves forward briskly, with a high 'density' of learner participation.

However, the very openness of the exercise and the emphasis on learner initiative may sometimes confuse and embarrass students who are more used to being told exactly what to say. In such cases it is important to define very clearly the kind of response required, and use the more confident and imaginative students to provide some initial examples. Also, participants may not know the words they need to contribute new ideas: so you can either supply these as requested, or provide a 'pool' of useful words at the beginning. But as far as possible, learners should be encouraged to make do with what they know.

Brainstorms can be given as written work as well, in class or for homework assignments; or written and oral work can be combined, as when learners are asked first to note down all the ideas they can think of and then to share them.

f) CHAIN

As in a brainstorm, instruction and an initial cue are given by the teacher, resulting in a large number of responses by the learners. The difference is that whereas in a brainstorm all these responses relate to the original cue, in a chain only the first does, and thereafter each learner utterance is made in response to the one before. The simplest form of this is question-and-answer: A asks B a question, who answers and then asks C something, using the same, or a parallel, formula:

A: What do you like doing in your free time, B?
B: I like dancing. What do you like doing, C?
C: I like playing tennis. What do you like doing, D? . . .

Like the brainstorm, this technique produces a high proportion of learner talk, while allowing the teacher to monitor. There is usually some flexibility of response, giving students a chance to express individuality (23.3 *Chain story*); but not always (11.3 *Detectives*). A variant is the 'cumulative chain', where each student has to repeat all the previous contributions, in order, before making his or her own addition (8.2 *Piling up stores*).

Even if the actual responses are fairly controlled in form, the inter-action in general is more learner-centred than in types previously mentioned; the students' attention is on each other rather than on the teacher or the board.

In writing, the chain technique provides a legitimate framework for a favourite (but usually disapproved-of) student pastime: passing notes. Papers are passed from one student to the next, each one contributing a further step to the story, description, or whatever (23.11 *Cooperative story*). The advantage of the written chain is that the whole result – often entertaining or aesthetically pleasing – is available at the end for public gloating.

Up to now in all the types of interaction described, only one learner has been speaking at a time, allowing the teacher to monitor all utterances. However, if several interactions are being carried on simultaneously in class, the amount of productive practice carried on is greatly increased – at the expense, obviously, of direct teacher control of learner language. Thus, interactions of this type are useful when you are fairly confident that learners can produce acceptable instances of the structure without prompting – if they think about it – and you want to provide a large volume of practice that will make them more fluent in its use.

g) FLUID PAIRS

The basic idea for a transaction-based exchange between two students is provided by the teacher, often in the form of a prescribed dialogue. Each learner performs only one transaction with any one partner, and then goes on to do the same with another. For example, in a beginner class, the simple dialogue:

A: Do you have ... ?
B: Yes, I do, here you are. / No, I'm sorry, I don't have any.

is used by 'buyers' and 'sellers' in a shopping simulation, as the 'buyers' move around trying to acquire the different items on their lists (8.6 *Shopping list*).

If the information provided in the exchange is based on individual tastes or opinions, then the same question will produce different answers with different people, so there is some point in asking it again. Some activities, for example, are based on doing a mini-survey (14.2 *Opinion questionnaire*): learners go from one to another of their classmates to find out the answers to their questions.

The fluid-pair technique provides an extremely useful framework for repetition – with a communicative purpose – of set questions or exchanges. It is another under-used one: in this case possibly because of the fear by teachers that the large amount of verbal interaction and physical movement will result in a loss of control. In my experience, however, students doing a fluid-pair exercise very rarely deviate from the task they have been set – though admittedly they can be very noisy: it is a good idea to have a bell or some other prearranged signal for stopping.

h) SEMI-CONTROLLED SMALL GROUP TRANSACTIONS

The teacher provides a 'skeleton' dialogue, or idea for a conversation, which the learners perform in pairs or small groups. The language to be produced by students is semi-controlled: that is to say, they are told to make use of certain patterns or kinds of sentences – but the exact content is left up to them. Usually such transactions are based on an information-gap task. For example, students may give each other directions or commands (25.4 *Describe and arrange*) or convey or request specified information (19.6 *Exam results*). This too can be done in writing, again through passing notes or short letters in a kind of intimate, immediate correspondence (31.3 *Written enquiries*).

This is a very effective type of activation for students who are well on the way to mastering the structure. You do, however, have to be very sure that they know what they have to do, and why, and that they have the language (lexical as well as grammatical) necessary to do it. Thus it is usually a good idea to do a preliminary full-class 'rehearsal' of the task before dividing students into groups to try it on their own.

i) FREE GROUP DISCUSSION

This is the least controlled form of interaction. The teacher gives a task, whose performance is likely to involve use of the grammatical structure being practised, and simply lets the students get on with it, with minimum intervention.

The size of the group can vary; it is usually bigger than that of *Semi-controlled small group transactions* as described above – and may even be the full class. Sometimes students move from one kind of grouping to another within the same activity, as when a task done in small groups is later assessed in a full class discussion.

Because of the relative lack of teacher control over what is said, this model is best used at the stage where the learners can be relied upon to produce acceptable forms of the structure in prescribed or controlled contexts, and you want to give them experience in using it more naturally and spontaneously in their own self-initiated speech.

What they will actually say is up to them: in theory, they may choose not to use the structure you want them to practise at all! But it is possible to design the discussion task in such a way that they are in fact very likely to do so; for example, a discussion task based on agreeing on a scale of priorities is likely to generate a good deal of use of the comparative (5.7 *Ranking*), whereas one based on discussing experience relevant to a present situation is likely to produce the present perfect (26.9 *The right experience for the job*). You may or may not wish to encourage your students to use the structure in question by frankly directing them to do so in advance; or you may draw their attention to instances as they occur. In any case, the structure is likely to occur less frequently than in other more controlled exercises, but more purposefully and naturally. This is perhaps the most advanced type of communicative grammar practice: if the students succeed in using the structure correctly and appropriately in group discussions, you can be fairly sure that they have mastered it – at least in its spoken form.

The follow-up, or parallel, in writing – though lacking the element of interaction – is the free creative essay; again it is up to you to choose a topic and setting that will be likely to generate use of the structures being practised. This brings us full circle back to the first of the techniques described in this section, since the kinds of texts presented to learners at the earliest stages of receptive practice are precisely those we may suggest they try to produce themselves at this, the most advanced level of language production.

4 In the classroom

This chapter deals with some practical aspects of the presentation and performance of grammar-practice activities in the classroom. The first section gives a series of practical hints for classroom teaching; and the second some suggestions for improving examples of specific coursebook exercises, using principles and techniques outlined in this and previous chapters.

1 Practical hints

a) LONG-TERM PLANNING

When planning a series of exercises for a particular grammar topic, it is very important to make sure that your programme is **varied**. That is to say, it should provide thorough 'coverage' of the different aspects of the structure (form and meaning-in-context, written and spoken modes); it should be based on varied topics and task-types; and it should provide opportunities for different types of student activation.

If your coursebook is a good one, it will do most of this planning for you – in fact, this is one of the criteria of what makes a good coursebook – but if not, you will need to supplement. For example, your book may give plenty of form-based exercises, but few meaning-based ones; or be composed of test-like items with no latitude for student initiative or invention; or the topics may be too limited; or there may be too little oral work. In such cases you may need to add activities you invent yourself or cull from books like this one (see BIBLIOGRAPHY), and omit some of the coursebook exercises to compensate.

b) SHORT-TERM PREPARATION

'Short-term preparation' means what you do to prepare for a specific lesson, usually not more than a few days (sometimes only a few hours, or less) before the lesson is due to take place.

Just selecting an exercise out of the coursebook – or out of this book, for that matter – and noting down the page number is not sufficient preparation. You will find that in order for grammar-practice activities to succeed it is best to have clear in your mind in advance, if not actually written down, most of the following points:

i) *Lesson context* At what point in the lesson will the activity take place? Is there any way I can link it to what went before or what is coming after? If not, how will I make sure that the transition from one activity to the next is smooth?

ii) *Introduction* Do I need to do a brief review of the grammar before launching into the practice activity, to ensure that the latter will be done successfully? How will I introduce the activity and define its objectives? What instructions will I need to give, in what language, as to how to do the task? Will I need to do a trial run or 'rehearsal' before starting the activity proper?

iii) *Supplementary materials* Do I need extra hardware, visuals, texts, or other supplementary material? If so, are they easily accessible, and not too many or elaborate for easy manipulation in the classroom?

iv) *Order* If the procedure is multi-stage, do I know exactly what comes after what? If there are follow-up activities, are they ready, with necessary material?

v) *Reserve* Do I have some extra activities ready, in case my prepared exercise cannot be used for some reason, or does not go well, or finishes earlier than expected?

vi) *Homework* Have I planned what homework, if any, I am going to give to reinforce the practice? And do I have the necessary information and instructions ready to give the students?

Most of these points are dealt with more fully later in this section.

c) INTRODUCTION

Before any classroom exercise you usually make some brief comments to introduce it. The most important thing here is clarity: as a result of the introduction, the students should know exactly what the objectives of the activity are, and how they are expected to achieve them. If the class is a monolingual and not very advanced one which finds it difficult and time-consuming to grapple with explanations in English, the introduction may often best be done in the students' native language (assuming you know it).

With younger classes it is not usually necessary to define exactly what the linguistic objective is ('The use of the modals of obligation', for example), though they should be aware of the general learning aim ('We're going to practise some words we've learnt'). But for more mature learners it is a good idea to let them know more precisely what you are going to practise with them: for one thing it helps them and you to feel that there is a sharing of the responsibility for learning; for another, they are more likely to make an effort if they know exactly what it is for. Very often, particularly in the more communicative and game-like activities, the language learning purpose is far from obvious; and if it is not explained, some students may feel they are wasting time doing them ('Why are we playing games instead of doing serious language work?').

The non-linguistic objective, if there is one, also has to be explained: to guess something, to convey information, and so on. If the activity is a game-like one, I am not – as I have mentioned before – usually in favour of stressing the idea that it is a 'game' when introducing it; grammar practice activities, however enjoyable, should usually be presented frankly as such. The exception is when both teacher and class really need a period of recreation and fun: as a temporary break during a period of very intense study for an exam, for example, or at the end of a long day, week or term.

If the class is to do any kind of independent (individual, group or pair) work in the process of the activity, it is vital for the **instructions** to be clearly given before they start. This is the weak point of many inexperienced teachers: they give instructions that are clear to themselves, and then launch into the activity without checking that the students are sure what they have to do. The result is very often that the teacher has to stop the activity in the middle to reissue instructions, or that there is delay and a constant distracting buzz of talk as students consult each other.

There are various ways of making sure that instructions are clear: by slowing down delivery, repeating, and/or using the students' native language; by doing a 'trial run', or demonstration of an activity with the full class before letting them work independently; by simply asking them, before setting them to work, if there is any unclear point they would like to ask about.

The instructions for an activity based on independent (individual, group or pair) work, incidentally, should usually include some provision for ending: how long the activity is expected to last, what the students should do after they finish, what happens if some finish early or late, what is to be done with any written or recorded results.

d) TIMING

The place of a grammar-practice activity is preferably in the middle of a lesson rather than right at the beginning or at the end. Students are freshest and most receptive at the beginning of the lesson: this is therefore the best time to present new language topics or texts, or to re-present difficult material. More extensive fluency practice tends to come later in the period. The end of the lesson I like to leave for 'rounding-off': reviewing what we have done, checking that everyone knows what is to be prepared at home, possibly a brief 'lightweight' activity involving not too much effort of concentration to give the session a pleasant finish.

This model is of course very generalized, and a basis for variation. Although as a rule grammar practice activities should be done soon after the beginning of a lesson, they may come right at the beginning if there is no new material to be presented, and you want to devote the students' energies mainly to the practice; and they may go on to the end if there is nothing else to be got through in the lesson, and the practice procedure is obviously a profitable one that is worth doing for as long as possible.

e) PACE

'Pace' is quite a different thing from 'speed'. An activity may be done quite slowly and still have pace, or quickly, yet lack it. If an exercise has pace, it means that the class is occupied with a steady flow of interesting stimuli to respond to, together with a feeling of constant progress towards the objective of the activity. If there are frequent interruptions, delays or digressions, the pace will flag, and the activity produce less volume of language practice and all the problems associated with boredom. But if the pace is too hurried, learners will not have time to absorb material and there will be a feeling of stress and restlessness. It will help if you:

i)   Have a clear lesson plan, so that you can make the transition from one item to the next, or from one activity to the next smoothly and briskly;
ii) Have all materials, including visuals, ready at hand, so that they can be manipulated without delay;
iii) Keep an eye on the clock so that the timing is balanced and you do not find yourself having to draw out one activity or rush another;
iv) Make sure you are aware of student reactions, so that you know whether the pace suits them, or whether you are going too fast or too slow for some of them;
v)   Try not to allow yourself to be deflected from the exercise for too long by discipline problems, problems of individuals, or attempts on the part of the students to change the subject; not always possible, admittedly, but in most cases the immediate problem can be dealt with summarily and/or postponed for future discussion, allowing you to maintain continuity.

f) SUPPLEMENTARY MATERIALS

Supplementary materials are all those things you bring to a classroom for a particular lesson, other than the routine books and equipment that are always present. They might consist of duplicated texts or exercises from another book, pictures or other visuals for display, sets of materials for group or pair work, or more sophisticated equipment such as overhead, film or slide projectors, tape recorders, or computers, with appropriate software.

The frequent use of such materials is likely to improve the quality of teaching: varied stimuli help to provide coverage of the different aspects of the structure, and add interest. It is usually worth making the effort to use some kind of supplementary item in most lessons; but there is such a thing as overdoing it! Some useful questions to ask yourself might be:

i) Do the materials I want to use really contribute to good learning in the practice I have planned? Are they essential to the performance of the exercise? If not, if I am using them for extra illustration or enrichment – are they clear, interesting and relevant to the topic, so that students will feel that they help, rather than being an unnecessary encumbrance or distraction?

ii) Are the materials ready at hand and easily manipulated? Have I laid them out, or set them up, before beginning the lesson so that I can start using them easily and quickly at the right moment? Have I checked that I have brought the right amount, so that I will not need to leaf through piles of pictures looking for the right one, or find myself short of duplicated sheets?

iii) If I am using electric equipment, have I prepared an alternative (material or reserve activity) in case there is a power failure or malfunction?

iv) If the material is bulky, heavy, elaborate, expensive or brought from a long distance – is it really cost-effective? That is to say, is the learning value my students will receive from the use of the material worth the investment of time, money and effort I put into getting hold of it? (Sometimes a difficult question to answer honestly, but one that needs to be faced: supplementary materials, however elaborate and attractive, are a means to an end, not an end in themselves.)

g) EXTENDING ACTIVITIES

Sometimes you may feel that an exercise has been a good one, but that there has been insufficient text or opportunity to engage with it – there has not been enough volume or repetition of the language practised. You feel you would like to do it again in order to give extra practice, but realize that simply repeating it will in most cases bore and irritate the class.

There are various ways of extending practice activities in order to provide the extra repetition; here are some of them.

i) *Repeating in a different mode* An exercise that has been done orally can then be redone in writing, or vice versa; for example, an exercise done for homework is often checked orally in class; or an exercise done in class subsequently given as written homework.

ii) *Repeating selectively* Some bits of the exercise can be selected for review; this lessens the boredom, since there is an element of the unexpected – the class does not know which items will be used. The teacher may select, or may ask students to do so: 'Choose a question you found difficult, see if you can do it now' or 'Choose something you're sure you know'; or even: 'Guess which question I'm thinking of.'

iii) *Recalling*   After an oral practice activity, students can be challenged to recall as much as they can of what was said. If, for example, a conventional discrete-item exercise was used, they can be asked to shut their books and try to remember all the items; if a brainstorm, when a large number of utterances have been heard, they may be asked to try to recall a defined number of sentences: 'Can you remember (at least) ten suggestions that have been made?' The recalling can be done orally or in writing, individually or in pairs or groups.

iv) *Editing*   After a written activity, students can get together and go through the exercise again in order to help each other correct and improve their work. If the exercise was not open-ended, groups of students can pool their efforts to produce a final joint version as correct as possible. If open-ended – that is to say, if each student has something different, as in essay-writing – then students can read their texts to each other, and exchange comments and advice.

v) *Composing*   Students can be invited to compose their own exercise(s) as a continuation of a textbook one, using the same kind of texts and task. They can then ask each other, or the entire class, to perform it. You can add further incentive by inviting students to improve on the interest, humour or drama of the original, or to adapt it to refer to their own circumstances or personalities.

vi) *Varying*   In 'matching' or slot-filling exercises, students are often asked to put together two components in order to form logical propositions. As a follow-up, you might suggest that they match incongruous components to make nonsense or humorous propositions (but still grammatical!) – and then possibly justify them or suggest situations where they might be true. Or they may simply invent their own 'fillers' to make original, personal, or amusing sentences.

h)   HOMEWORK

Homework, as suggested above, is a useful way of extending classroom exercises, giving an opportunity to review the material. This is probably its primary function; a secondary one is to serve as an informal test, providing the teacher with useful feedback as to how well the material has been mastered. Very occasionally we may wish to give totally fresh material for homework, as a preliminary to a new topic, or just for a change.

Students usually do their homework on their own: home assignments should therefore be slightly easier than classroom ones, where teacher assistance is available. For the same reason, you should take great care over the giving of instructions for homework – misunderstandings cannot be cleared up once the students have left the classroom. I like to give homework in the middle of the lesson rather than at the end, thus leaving myself plenty of time to explain and iron out problems; at the end of the lesson all I will need to do is put in a brief reminder.

The checking of grammar exercises done for homework is a tedious chore for the teacher if done by taking in notebooks and correcting at home; but it is often equally tedious for students if done orally in class, besides taking up valuable lesson time that would often be better employed doing new exercises. In principle, homework should be checked in class only if there is real learning value to be got out of doing so – that is to say, if the homework review actually functions as an effective practice procedure in itself, fulfilling the criteria described in Chapter 2. Otherwise – time permitting – you should check individual assignments after class. The process may be made less arduous by asking students to do some preliminary correcting of each other's work before giving it in; this in itself can be a useful technique for awareness-raising.

The main point is, of course, that you should relate to and give feedback on home assignments in some way as soon as possible after they are done. If you ignore students' homework or only look at it weeks after it is done, they soon get the message that you do not care about it too much, and cease to invest effort in it. Also, of course, the comments you make on home assignments provide a valuable opportunity for relating to individuals with appropriate criticism, praise or encouragement – something you often have no time for in a big class during lesson time.

i) RECORDS

It is a good idea to keep some sort of record of teaching ideas for grammar practice that have worked. I am not in favour of preserving lesson plans: these are bulky, often untidy, and much of their substance has no value beyond the actual lesson they were written for. But before throwing them out, it is worth going through them and picking out particular bits that you remember as being successful. These can then be noted on cards and filed in a card index under grammatical headings. The time spent on making and adding to a card index of this type is well repaid when you come to teach the same structure next time.

2 Getting the most out of coursebook exercises

In this section I shall look critically at four grammar exercises which I feel represent types of exercises we are often called upon to teach in the classroom, and consider what could be done to exploit their texts or tasks to provide maximally effective practice. A number of supplementary procedures are suggested for each exercise – but it is not, of course, implied that all these should be implemented when actually presenting similar exercises in class! – they are merely possible options, to be used selectively. Different ideas are given for each exercise, though you may notice that a procedure suggested for one of them could sometimes apply equally well to another.

a) THE FUTURE TENSE

1	When will you meet Ronald?	Maybe I'll meet him on Sunday.
2	.... Maggie come round?	.... tonight.
3	.... Thomas go away?	.... Friday evening.
4	.... we move house?	.... next year.
5	.... you telephone?	.... sometime next week.
6	.... Jon and Tim arrive?	.... soon.

This exercise gives practice in the interrogative and declarative forms of the verb with *will*, to express expected events at a defined time in the future. The learner is asked to insert the missing words, which include the tense to be practised, into disconnected sentences, and is given an example at the beginning which provides a reliable model for the rest of the items. The actual meaning of the sentences is not very important, the emphasis being on correct forms. Answers may be given in speech or in writing.

As it stands, this exercise is a little boring and rather short; let us consider what could be done to give it more interest and volume.

One of the reasons for the lack of interest is the fact that the characters are anonymous, and the relationships undefined. You could discuss with the class who the various characters are and what the relationships between them might be; or you could bring to the class pictures cut out of magazines purporting to represent the different people – which has the added advantage of providing a visual focus; or you could simply invite them to substitute names of members of the class for the names given. Any of these will immediately make the exercise more meaningful.

Another reason for lack of interest is the fact that the answers are prescribed. I would probably tell my class to ignore the answer cues ('...tonight'), or use them only to help think up ideas of their own as to when the various things will happen. If the characters are renamed to correspond to people the students know, then the answers can also correspond to real forthcoming events:

A: When will you meet Pablo?

B: (Maybe) I'll meet him after the lesson.

Further variations can be added to the exercise to give extra volume: for example, other question words can be substituted for *When* at the beginning of each question, and answers given in the future:

A: Where will you meet Pablo?

B: I'll see him in the cafeteria.

A: Why will Maria telephone?

B: She'll telephone to tell us why she didn't come today.

You might then ask the students to suggest further developments to each item in answer to the question: 'What will (probably) happen then?'

Later they can even try – individually or in groups – to invent an entire programme of future happenings that will somehow include and link together all the events described in the exercise.

b) VERB+ING WITH PREPOSITION

He congratulated him	stealing the money.
They blamed the students	being impolite.
He did not forgive her	passing the test.
I apologised	making the mistake.
We praised the girls	forgetting to come.
The teacher punished him	causing an accident.
He accused the young man	succeeding.

Example: We praised the girls for succeeding.

The learners are asked to pair phrases from the left-hand column with ones in the right-hand column to make logical sentences, inserting appropriate prepositions in the middle. Unlike the previous exercise, the given example does not provide a reliable model for all the rest, as the prepositions vary: the 'pre-learning' aspect is not built in, and without proper preparation this exercise might only produce a series of mistakes, functioning as a test rather than a practice. The sentences have some interesting ideas in them, but there is not really enough volume and repetition of the structure.

I would introduce this exercise by reminding the class which verbs take which prepositions, and giving a few examples, in order to make it more likely that students will afterwards do the exercise itself successfully. After first doing the exercise orally, using individual volunteers to suggest answers, extra contextual interest could be added by asking the students to continue each sentence with an explanation, for example:

We praised the girls for succeeding – it was a very difficult test, and they had worked at it very hard.

Another possibility is to ask students to combine incongruous components, to make sentences like:

>He congratulated him on stealing the money.

and then again adding justification:

>He congratulated him on stealing the money – which was really his, anyway.

Later, students can be asked to take only the introductory phrases and invent their own endings, possibly in writing for homework. Alternatively, they can be asked to use the first person ('I praised', 'I congratulated', etc.) and compose sentences that describe real personal experiences, with or without explanatory notes. Such open-ended tasks can produce interesting results, which students may enjoy sharing later.

c) THE INTERROGATIVE

Ask him who he is.
Who are you?

1 Ask him where he lives.
2 Ask him how long it takes him to come to work.
3 Ask him when he came to live here.
4 Ask him what he likes to read.
5 Ask him who he is looking at.
6 Ask him how many brothers and sisters he has.

This is in fact a transformation exercise: students are asked to put indirect questions into direct speech. It could be done in conventional teacher-student exchanges round the class, or in pairs, or individually in writing. Again the subject matter is rather uninteresting and completely decontextualized. Also, its coverage is rather limited: it concentrates on the third person singular – masculine only! – which goes into the second person in the direct question – and on the present simple; other tenses have only token representation. The rules governing the transformation of statements into questions vary according to the tense and aspect of the verb; so that the first example does not help very much. Also, there is no apparent provision made for answering the questions – most of which seem a little pointless.

I would probably use the actual text of this exercise as a basis for a review (re-presentation) of the rules for forming questions in the different tenses, rather than as a practice procedure itself, and then go on to get the students to compose further similar exercises to provide better coverage and more interest.

One way this can be done is by adapting the exercise to form the basis for interview simulation. Students could be told that they are editors giving instructions to reporters about what questions to ask when interviewing a certain celebrity ('Ask him or her...'). The questions should cover the celebrity's past and present occupations and future plans and his or her opinions about other people and events. The whole class can be given the same celebrity – or a choice – or each student can be given a different name; and the work may be done individually or in small groups or pairs. Some real or imaginary celebrities that could be used: a famous film or pop star; a controversial local political figure; visitors from outer space; a talking elephant; the founder of a new religion; a mother of 20 children; a man aged 100; the owner of an unusual pet; and so on. The prepared questions could then be used in role-plays of the interviews; or the direct question forms could be written out in the form of questionnaires and exchanged for answering in a kind of written role-play procedure. Alternatively, individual students could be given the celebrity roles in advance and told that they may choose what to be asked in the interview; their exercises will then be based on the format 'Ask me...'; again, the follow-up would consist of a role-play of the actual interview.

d) THE POSSESSIVE 'S

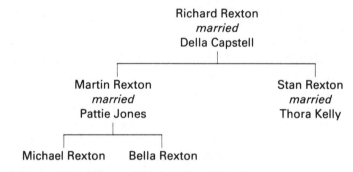

Richard Rexton
married
Della Capstell

Martin Rexton
married
Pattie Jones

Stan Rexton
married
Thora Kelly

Michael Rexton   Bella Rexton

Martin Rexton – Stan Rexton: *Martin is Stan's brother.*
Stan Rexton – the children: *Stan is the children's uncle.*

1 Richard Rexton – Della Capstell   5 Martin – Richard
2 Martin Rexton – Bella Rexton   6 Thora Kelly – Richard
3 Michael Rexton – Bella   7 Pattie Jones – Martin Rexton
4 Stan Rexton – the children   8 Della Capstell – Stan Rexton

A description of family relationships is a good overall context for the use of the possessive 's, and the family tree itself provides an excellent visual focus. The names, however, are a little long and consonant-clustered, and the family lacks 'reality'. Also, the numbered questions are rather rigid, leaving no latitude for student choice or initiative.

Having reviewed names of family members (father, aunt, sister, etc.) and made clear how sentences about family relationships using 's can be derived from the diagram, I would probably abandon questions 1–8 completely, and instead invite students to find and express as many relationships illustrated in the diagram as they can, in any order they like. If the diagram is on the board or OHP, coloured arrows can be drawn to indicate relationships that the students have defined. Later you can point to an arrow and ask students to reconstruct the sentence that produced it; or number the arrows and ask them to write an appropriate sentence for each one.

The problem of the heavy names can of course be solved by simply omitting surnames; but the family remains somewhat anonymous, even if you depict the different characters using magazine pictures. Perhaps a real family could be substituted – a famous one like the British royal family, or a locally well-known one; alternatively you could use characters from a television series currently being shown; or your own family; or that of one of the students (with prior permission, of course!). In all these cases, photographs can also be used, with the advantage that they are of 'real' identifiable people.

For further practice, students can be divided into pairs for an information-gap exercise. Each student has a family-tree diagram, with different names missing; students supply each other with the missing information in answer to questions. Or the family tree can be expressed as a written description of the relationships, which is then used to reconstruct the original diagram. This can be done also in oral pair work: one student describes the relationships while the other listens and draws the family tree. Students can be asked to describe their own families to each other in this way, which adds personal involvement; but in this case, you should try to make sure in advance that no one would be distressed by having to do so – the subject can occasionally be a sensitive one. In all such relatively free variations, you may find that you need to remind, or help, students to use the *'s* as they interact.

PART TWO: ACTIVITIES

1 Adjectives

(For comparatives and superlatives see under *Comparison of adjectives*, page 62.)

1.1 Finding twins

Position of adjective(s) before noun. Simple reading, controlled speaking and writing.

Materials: Individual copies of a grid showing several alternative adjective–noun combinations within a sentence, as in *Box 1*.

Procedure: Each student marks off one option in each column – according to his or her own tastes, or at random. Then each tries to find someone else with exactly the same choices by asking others:

Do you have a big white cat?

Do you like romantic novels, folk music and comedy films?

Some students may find no 'twins'; some may find several. In any case, the search process goes on until all the students have spoken to one another (if practical! – otherwise until you call a halt).

BOX 1

Adjective–noun combinations

I have a ...

big	black	dog
small	brown	mouse
fat	white	cat

I have some ...

expensive	French	paintings
cheap	Spanish	vases
rare	Italian	glasses

I like ...

detective		modern		historical		
romantic	novels,	classical	music and	horror	films.	
science-fiction		folk		comedy		

© Cambridge University Press 1988

1.2 Guessing adjectival phrases

Position of adjective before noun. Free oral guessing, based on given noun.

Materials: A set of ten or so cards or slips of paper on each of which an adjective–noun phrase is written, as in *Box 2.*

Procedure: One student is given a phrase, and tells the others only what the noun is. They then have to guess the entire phrase. For example, if the 'knower' gives the noun *table*, the others might guess:

A square table?

A small table?

A wooden table?

You may need to give hints to facilitate guessing, tell them when they are getting 'warm', and so on. The one who guesses the correct solution gets the next phrase to be guessed.

Variations: Later, the students think up their own combinations for guessing – preferably based on a real object or person.

Comment: Remember to insist on the students using the entire phrase or sentence when making their guesses. Just saying 'big?' or 'square?' gives no practice in the adjective-before-noun construction.

BOX 2

Guessing adjectives

1 A tall man	2 A fat baby	3 A brown cow
4 A happy girl	5 A wooden table	6 A square suitcase
7 A cotton tablecloth	8 An exciting film	9 A long story
10 A soft bed	11 A red light	12 A boring book

© Cambridge University Press 1988

1.3 Inserting adjectives

Position and meaning of adjective before noun. Oral responses to heard text; or written responses to reading.

Materials: A story or other interesting text of 100–300 words with few or no adjectives. You could improvise it from notes, read it aloud from a full text, or present it in written form. Probably the best source is your coursebook; or you can use books of short stories (see BIBLIOGRAPHY). If it is a ready-made text, you might need to delete adjectives before presenting it for use here – but in most cases this is probably unnecessary: there are enough unmodified nouns in most texts for the purposes of this activity.

Procedure: Read or improvise the text aloud, stopping at appropriate nouns for the students to volunteer ideas for descriptive adjectives that might go with them. Alternatively, present only the written form of the text with blank spaces where students are to insert adjectives.

Variations: You can give a written text with no obvious blanks. The students then have to identify the nouns and the right place for the adjective by themselves, making the exercise rather more advanced and challenging.

An amusing variation is to ask students to supply adjectives **without** knowing what the context is or what they are describing. You write in the adjective, however unsuitable, and then read out or display the result at the end. This, however, gives only receptive practice in positioning the adjective.

Comment: You may wish to provide a set of adjectives in advance for students to choose from; this makes the procedure easier, but lessens its heterogeneity and interest.

See also:
3.2 *Cooperative poem*;
7.1 *Defining by sense*;
8.2 *Piling up stores*, if the 'piling up' consists of a collection of adjective + noun combinations, starting with a cue-sentence like 'When I go shopping I must buy a black pen . . .';
15.5 *Common denominator*, if the 'denominator' is defined by an adjective.

2 Adverbs

2.1 Miming adverbs

Formation of adverbs with -*ly*; oral guesses.

Procedure: Select a manner adverb (e.g. *slowly*, *secretly*), and tell all the class but one what it is. The one who does not know gives a command to one of the others – for example:

Get up and turn round!

If the adverb chosen has been *slowly*, then the student will do the action slowly. If the guesser cannot yet identify the adverb, he or she will give another command to someone else – and so on, until the word is guessed or revealed.

2.2 Miming sentences with adverbs

Position of manner adverbs in the sentence. Oral guessing, based on cue cards.

Materials: One set of cue cards with manner adverbs on them, another with short sentences describing actions that can be mimed – all based on vocabulary known to the class (examples in *Box 3*).

Procedure: A student takes one adverb and one verb, and mimes the combination (e.g. *catch a ball* + *lovingly*). The others have to guess what was on the two cards, formulated in a grammatical sentence:

You are catching / you caught a ball lovingly!

BOX 3

Guessing actions and adverbs

1 SLOWLY	a) TURN ON A TELEVISION
2 HAPPILY	b) DRINK A CUP OF TEA
3 NERVOUSLY	c) CLIMB A TREE
4 HEAVILY	d) CLEAN A WINDOW
5 ANGRILY	e) PUT ON A SHIRT
6 LOVINGLY	f) MAKE A BED
7 GENTLY	g) CATCH A BALL
8 VIOLENTLY	h) TYPE A LETTER

2.3 Frequency surveys

Position of frequency adverbs in sentence; inserting adverbs into spoken or written sentences.

Materials: Individual copies of questionnaire sheets, beginning *How often...?*, followed by a series of questions. For example, students may be asked how often a good teacher they have known gave homework, played games, etc.; or they may answer questions on television-viewing habits. Answers may be filled in by ticking columns (*Box 4a*) or by noting down number codes (*Box 4b*).

Procedure: Go through questionnaires making sure all questions, and

---

BOX 4a

Frequency surveys (1)

A good teacher I have known

How often did he or she ...

	always	very often	often	sometimes	rarely	never
1 ... give homework?						
2 ... play games?						
3 ... make jokes?						
4 ... give punishments?						
5 ... praise?						
6 ... criticize?						
7 ... get angry?						
8 ... smile?						

Now fill in the grid again for *A bad teacher I have known!*

© Cambridge University Press 1988

instructions, are understood. Then students fill in their own question-naires individually, or work in pairs, asking each other 'How often did he or she / do you ... ?'. Afterwards they report results using full sentences:

I always watch television at weekends.

Henri's teacher sometimes gave homework.

This may be done either orally, in response to your questions:

What answers did you get to the first question?

What are Jacqueline's viewing habits?

or in writing, for homework.

Comment: Make clear what you mean by *always* (every day?) *sometimes* (twice a week? twice a month? every other day?), etc., otherwise students may have difficulty deciding what to answer.

BOX 4b

Frequency surveys (2)

Television-watching habits

By each question fill in a number:

1=never   2=seldom   3=occasionally   4=often   5=always

How often do you ...

1 ... watch television on a weekday? ....

2 ... watch television at the weekend? ....

3 ... leave the television on even if you are doing something else?
....

4 ...turn the television on automatically when you come home?
....

5 ... feel guilty about watching too much television?
....

6 ... limit yourself to a certain number of hours' viewing? ....

7 ... look up programmes in advance to find things you'll enjoy?
....

8 ... watch programmes alone? ....

9 ... turn the television off if visitors come? ....

10 ... feel that watching a certain programme was really worth-while? ....

© Cambridge University Press 1988

2.4   What do you do when ... ?

Position of frequency adverbs; free composition of sentences, oral or written.

Procedure: Ask students a cue question like 'What do you do when you are depressed?' and ask them to jot down a few ideas, using one of the frequency adverbs *always, usually, often, sometimes* each time:

    I sometimes go out and buy some new clothes.
    I usually just sit and listen to music.

Then share ideas with each other; or try to find other students who have similar reactions.

Variations: Alternative situations that can provide cues are: other moods (when you are happy, annoyed, bored, nervous) or events (when you have a free day, quarrel with a friend, have an exam the next day, find yourself short of money).

See also:
1.3   *Inserting adjectives*, using adverbs instead of adjectives;
23.3   *Chain story*, using adverbs for the cues;
28.3   *Routines.*

3 Articles, definite and indefinite

(For *a/an* contrasted with *some* see under *Countable/uncountable, singular/plural nouns*, page 86.)

3.1 Expanding headlines

Use of appropriate article in noun phrase; inserting *a/an/the* into headline; oral or written.

Materials: A pile of English-language newspapers, or headlines cut out from them.

Procedure: Ask the students to go through the headlines they have, inserting *a/an/the*, or leaving no article, where they feel appropriate. Do a few examples with them; then let them carry on alone (or in pairs or small groups). You may need to help individuals with comprehension occasionally. Then check answers yourself; or ask them to check each other's answers consulting you in cases of doubt.

Variations: Later, you may ask students to insert not only missing articles, but also auxiliary verbs that are often omitted (*is/are, do/does/did*), or any other items necessary to form complete sentences.

Sometimes there are cases where two, or any, of the three alternative articles (*the* or *a/an* or nothing) are possible. It can be interesting to discuss what difference these variations make to the sense, or implications, of the headline.

3.2 Cooperative poem

Use of appropriate article; free composition of noun phrases in writing.

Procedure: Give the students a title of a poem: something which is likely to be rich in associations and connotations, like 'Night' or 'Home' or 'The Sea'. You might take the title from literature you have read recently in class, or some topical association; or ask students to suggest one.

Invite students to write a noun phrase describing an association the topic has for them. Then write up suggestions on the board. 'Night', for

example, might produce:
> Darkness.
> An owl calling.
> The world at rest.

The result is a sort of impressionistic poem.

The contributions may be made richer if students are allowed to add a word or two to each such phrase – a prepositional phrase, an adverb, a verb; for example:
> Darkness over everything.
> An owl calls in the distance.
> The world is at rest.

but the basis remains the noun phrase.

Variations: Each student has a loose sheet of paper and is given or (better) chooses an individual topic, which he or she writes at the top of the page. He or she then writes the first line of the poem, as suggested above, and passes the paper to a neighbour. The neighbour continues with a second line – and so on. Papers may be left open throughout, so that every new contributor can see everything that has been written before; or folded, leaving visible only one previous line.

The results may then be read out to the class, or, having been checked and corrected by you, copied out and displayed.

See also:

1.3 *Inserting adjectives*, inserting articles as well as adjectives.

4 Both ... and, either ... or, neither ... nor

4.1 Association dominoes

Position of *both* before verb or after *are*; free oral responses.

Materials: A large number of pictures of readily recognizable objects, animals, people – enough for each student to have at least three. You could use copies of pictures in *Box 5* or published sets of small pictures for language learning (see BIBLIOGRAPHY).

Procedure: Give each student two or three pictures, and stick one in the centre of the board with blu-tack. Any student may give you one of his or her pictures for sticking next to the central picture, provided he or she can suggest a convincing point of similarity. For example:

> A table may be stuck next to a dog because: they both have four legs.
> Or a pencil may go by a table because: they are both made of wood.

Some similarities suggested by students may be a bit farfetched; in cases of uncertainty, you decide whether to accept a particular link or not.

The same kind of similarity may not be used twice; for example, having linked a bag and a car with 'They are both used to carry things', another student may not use the same sentence to link, say, a horse with the car.

Students should make do with vocabulary they know, rather than asking you for new words.

The activity may be presented as a competition (the first five students to get rid of their pictures are the winners). Or (as I prefer) the objective may be to form an unbroken line of pictures from one end of the board to the other. In this case, students who run out of pictures should be given new ones from a reserve pile.

Variations: The same may be done later in small groups. Here, the rules are similar to those of conventional 'dominoes'.

BOX 5

Small pictures

BOX 5 continued

© Cambridge University Press 1988

4.2 Similarities

Use of *both ... and*, *neither ... nor* to describe similarities; constructing sentences based on grid, written or oral.

Materials: Individual copies of a grid showing what different people do, as in *Box 6a*.

Procedure: Invite students to find pairs of people with similarities:

> Both Elizabeth and Peter eat ice cream.
> Neither Roger nor Mary eat fish.

After a little full-class practice, pairs or groups of students may compete (against each other or against you) to see who can find most such 'twins'. They may be asked to write down their sentences.

BOX 6a

Similarities (1)

1 *What they eat (✓) or don't eat (×)*

	meat	ice cream	fish	tropical fruit	salad	pasta
Mary	✓	×	×	✓	✓	×
Peter	✓	✓	×	✓	×	×
Roger	×	×	×	✓	✓	✓
Elizabeth	×	✓	✓	×	×	✓

2 *What they can (✓) or can't (×) do*

	drive	speak two languages	type	play an instrument	swim
Tony	×	✓	✓	✓	×
Jeff	✓	✓	×	×	✓
Sue	×	×	✓	×	✓
Heather	✓	×	✓	✓	×
Brenda	✓	×	×	✓	✓

© Cambridge University Press 1988

Variations: In pairs, students each get different partially filled grids (*Box 6b*) and help each other to fill them in by describing who is similar to whom in what respect. They may not show each other their grids, and are only allowed to use sentences with *both ... and* or *neither ... nor*.

To practise *both* or *neither* alone, call out two names, and ask the class to identify a point of similarity between them:

Both (of them) eat fish.

Neither (of them) can type.

BOX 6b

Similarities (2)

Student A can

	drive	speak two languages	type	play an instrument	swim
Tony	✗	✓	✓	✓	✗
Jeff		✓			
Sue	✗		✓		
Heather				✓	✗
Brenda		✗		✓	✓

Student B can

	drive	speak two languages	type	play an instrument	swim
Tony					
Jeff	✓		✗	✗	✓
Sue		✗	✓	✗	✓
Heather	✓	✗	✓	✓	
Brenda	✓	✗	✗		

4.3 Possible candidates

Use of *either ... or* and *neither ... nor* to describe possible or impossible alternatives (also, *none of...*, *any of...*); constructing written or spoken sentences based on brief cues.

Materials: Brief descriptions of the qualifications of four or five people, and jobs they might be asked to do, as in *Box 7*. These may be displayed on the overhead projector, or individual copies distributed to students.

Procedure: Ask students to tell you which of the people described might or might not be able to cope with each job, using *either ... or* or *neither ... nor*.

Either Ali or Anita could cook a meal.

Neither Mark nor Christine could move heavy furniture.

This could also be done in pairs, or individually in writing.

Variations: You might ask students to think about members of the class: can they think of two people, either of whom is qualified to do a certain job? Use the jobs suggested in *Box 7* as a starting point, then encourage students to think of others.

See also:
28.8 *Things in common.*

BOX 7

> **Who could ... ?**
>
> 1 ... help move heavy furniture?
> 2 ... sing the treble (high) part in a song?
> 3 ... advise you about University studies?
> 4 ... cook a meal?
> 5 ... entertain a Spanish visitor?
> 6 ... drive you to the airport?
> 7 ... teach you to ride?
> 8 ... entertain an Arabic-speaking guest?
> 9 ... play in a basketball match?
> 10 ... paint a picture?

BOX 7 continued

CHRISTINE
Age: 10. Home: a Texas ranch.
Very musical (plays violin).
Speaks Spanish and English.
Hobbies: helping with the
horses, sports.

MARK
Age: 70. Home: Cairo.
Retired University professor.
Has had polio – in wheelchair.
Hobbies: painting, driving (in
special car).

ALI
Age: 24. Home: Morocco.
Works as chef in restaurant.
No driving licence.
Hobbies: riding, no other
sports.

ANITA
Age: 30. Home: Argentina.
Has M.A. in English. Musical,
artistic.
Allergic to animals.
Hobbies: cooking, ball games,
body-building.

5 Comparison of adjectives

5.1 Looking at advertisements

Understanding comparative and superlative adjectives in context; mainly reading.

Materials: A large number of English-language newspapers or magazines with plenty of advertisements in them; alternatively, a number of ready cut-out advertisements.

Procedure: Give each student, or pair of students, a pile of advertisements or periodicals, ask them to look through them to find instances of the comparative and/or superlative of adjectives. Help with comprehension where necessary. Each example when found may be highlighted with a fluorescent pen, or copied into a notebook.

Variations: The marked or copied sentences are later read out to the rest of the class, who have to guess what product was being advertised.

5.2 Making advertisements

Use of comparatives and superlatives in advertisements: free or cued writing.

Procedure: Preferably after doing *Looking at advertisements*, above, tell the students that they have to compose their own advertisement for a product (some ideas in *Box 8*), using comparative and superlative adjectives. They have to write it up neatly; and – optionally – design the layout and illustration. The results, when you have checked them, may be copied neatly and posted on the wall to decorate the classroom. Best done in pairs or groups.

Variations: The advertisement may be designed to be later read aloud or acted, like a television commercial.

The activity may be presented as a competition: the group which makes the best advertisement – written or spoken – is the winner.

BOX 8

Things you could advertise

1 *Imaginary products*
   Marve margarine; Supremo car; Wisdom computers; Sparkle cleaning fluid; Sleepo beds; Yummy chocolates; Vita vitamin pills.

2 *Local attractions*
   A local beauty spot; our school/college; a local newspaper; a forthcoming party/festive event; a local dish; a local product; a celebrity, or locally well-known personality.

3 *People and pets*
   Marriageable young man/woman (described by matchmaker); pet animal (advertised by pet shop);
   actor/singer/dancer (promoted by theatrical agency);
   au pair/cook/nanny/housekeeper (advertised by domestic help agency).

5.3 Brainstorming comparisons

Use of comparative and superlative adjectives, also *as . . . as* and *not so . . . as* to compare subjects; oral brainstorming based on set pattern.

Procedure: Give the students three names of objects (or animals, or professions, or whatever you like – examples in *Box 9*), and ask them to find as many points of comparison between the items as they can. For example, if they are given *a garden rake, a ball, a pencil*, comparisons might run:
   The pencil is smaller than the rake.
   The ball is the roundest.
   The pencil is more useful than the ball.
After a preliminary trial run with the whole class, another set of words can be given to small groups, who compete to see who can think of the most comparisons in three or four minutes. Encourage them to make do with vocabulary they know, rather than asking you for extra words.
   A similar task can be set for individual writing, or homework.
Variations: When students know each other fairly well, they can be put

into pairs and asked to compose sentences comparing themselves with each other:

> I am taller than you are.
>
> You speak more languages than I do.

Pairs may then be asked to write together a summary of their comparisons.

Comment: This activity can be used to practise any kind of comparing; but you can, of course, limit it to any particular construction you want when you give the preliminary instructions: the comparative with *-er than*, for example.

BOX 9

Things to compare

1 a pencil, a ball, a garden rake
2 an elephant, a snake, a crocodile
3 a television, a lamp, a chair
4 a rock, a mountain, a river
5 a car, an aeroplane, a bicycle

5.4 Comparing pictures

Use of comparative and superlative adjectives, also *as . . . as, not so . . . as,* to compare subjects; oral brainstorming based on set pattern.

Procedure: The students compare two or three pictures, which should have some theme in common. Some examples are given in *Box 10*; or you can use pictures from your coursebook, or cut out from magazines. The comparisons are likely to be longer and more complex than those produced in the previous activity. Students may relate to items within the picture:

> The girl in Picture 1A is prettier than the girl in Picture 1B.

or to the picture as a whole:

> Picture 1B is the darkest.

Again, this can be done as a group competition, with a time limit.

BOX 10

Pictures to compare

BOX 10   continued

3 A

B

C

BOX 10   continued

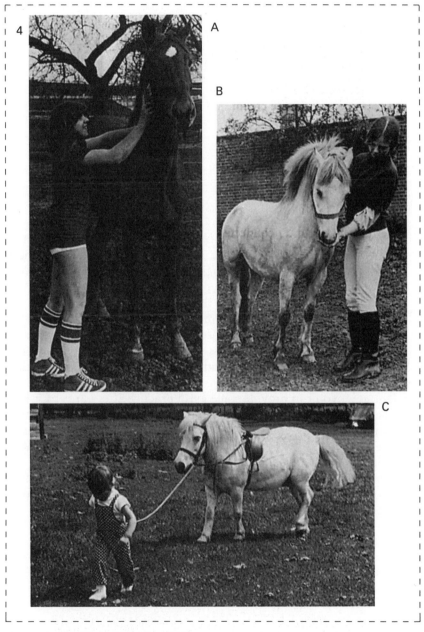

5.5 Circle comparisons

Use of comparative adjectives to compare subjects, based on single-word cues. Oral brainstorming based on set pattern; possible written follow-up.

Procedure: Show the students several nouns laid out in a rough circle thus:

macaroni

ice cream   apples

yoghurt   salt

water   curry

fish

The nouns should be connected in sense to a common theme (more examples in *Box 11*). They can be displayed on the board or overhead projector. Then ask students to suggest a point of comparison between any two; for example:

Ice cream is more fattening than yoghurt.

Draw a line between 'ice cream' and 'yoghurt' to represent the comparison, and ask for another sentence linking two other items ... and so on, until there is a criss-cross of lines linking the words. Participants should make do with known vocabulary, rather than asking you for new words.

Variations: You can provide some extra practice afterwards by asking students to recall sentences that are represented by the lines. Point to one line, and ask the class what was said when it was drawn in; when a student repeats the sentence, you delete the line – and so on, until all the lines are gone.

Later, students may be given sets of nouns on paper to work on individually, drawing in the lines and writing the corresponding sentences below.

BOX 11

Circle comparatives and superlatives

boots coat dress shirt hat watch umbrella jeans	lion spider snake cat mouse fly fish man
reading swimming sleeping watching TV eating driving dancing studying	hairdresser bus-driver housewife secretary pilot teacher mechanic doctor
field wood river city village sea lake mountain	car train plane spaceship bicycle ship skis submarine

(Or the students' own selection of names of local places, celebrities, television programmes, etc.)

© Cambridge University Press 1988

5.6   Circle superlatives

Use of superlatives to distinguish one of a set of cues; oral responses based on set pattern; optional written follow-up.

Procedure: Give the students circles of nouns as in *Box 11*, and ask them to take each member of the set in turn and find some respect in which it is superior (or inferior) to all the rest:

Macaroni is the most fattening.

Fish is the richest in protein.

They can later be given another set to work on individually, writing down one sentence for each item.

Activities

5.7 Ranking

Use of comparative adjectives, *as ... as*, *not so ... as*, to rank items on a scale. Spoken and written responses to cues, free discussion.

Materials: Sets of five or six linked nouns, and another four or five adjectives that express criteria that might be applied to them. For example, some of the foods suggested in *Circle comparisons* might be given criteria like *fattening, sweet, healthy, cheap.* The nouns and adjectives are laid out in the form of a grid (*Box 12*) and presented to the class on individual worksheets, on the board, or on the overhead projector.

Procedure: Check that the meanings of all the nouns and adjectives are known. Then students discuss in what order the items should be rated under each criterion. For example, if they think that macaroni is the most fattening, then they will insert the number '1' in the appropriate column by *macaroni*. Then, by discussing which of the other items is more or less fattening, they will decide on a final order. And so on, with all the other criteria, until the grid is filled.

Variations: This activity is suitable for group work. Each group is given the same grid to work on; later, results are compared, and the class tries to reach a final consensus (almost impossible, in my experience, but there is a lot of language practice to be got in the attempt!).

BOX 12

Ranking

	cheap	tasty	healthy	fattening	essential to life
macaroni					
water					
yoghurt					
curry					
arsenic					

BOX 12 continued

	strong	rare	intelligent	beautiful	dangerous
lions					
snakes					
men					
dogs					
spiders					

	healthy	tiring	productive	enjoyable
watching TV				
swimming				
driving				
studying				
sleeping				

5.8 Preferences

Use of comparative adjectives and *as ... as, not so ... as* to express preferences; inserting varied adjectives into fairly controlled sentence patterns; mostly oral.

Procedure: Present a set of two or three words, expressing concepts that are likely to arouse definite positive or negative reactions (some ideas in *Box 13*). Ask students to express and justify their preferences. For example:

> I prefer snakes to spiders because they are more colourful and graceful.
>
> I prefer a lake to a waterfall because it is quieter.

This may be done in open class discussion, in groups, or individually in writing; if the last, then results can be shared later. The aim is to find out what most members of the class prefer, possibly comparing their tastes to yours.

Variations: Each student chooses his or her own set of 'concepts', and goes round asking all the others which they prefer and why. In this way, all students are activated simultaneously, either asking or answering in a 'fluid pair' procedure. They can be asked to draw conclusions as to the tastes and reasons of the majority, which may be interesting to share with the rest of the class at the end.

Comment: You might like to use for the basic 'concepts' things you have been studying recently in class: new vocabulary, characters from literature you have read, etc.

BOX 13

Which do you prefer, and why?

1 snake, crocodile, spider
2 mud, sand, rock
3 dog, cat, canary
4 morning, afternoon, evening
5 summer, winter, (spring, autumn)
6 countryside, city, village
7 swimming, dancing, running
8 sweet, savoury, spicy food
9 pop, classical, folk music
10 waterfall, sea, lake

5.9 Quizzes

Use of comparative and superlative adjectives in questions (quizzes); understanding, responding to and composing such questions; mostly reading and writing.

Materials: Quizzes based on comparisons:
What is the highest mountain in the world?
Which is longer, the Amazon or the Nile?
More examples of questions using the comparative in *Box 14a*; superlative in *Box 14b*. Vocabulary should be familiar to the students, or easily guessed.

Procedure: Students answer the questions either orally or in writing, preferably in complete sentences:
Mount Everest is the highest mountain in the world.
They then make up their own quizzes, for each other to do.

Variation: Give the students only a name (Mount Everest; the Dead Sea; Queen Victoria) – and ask them to say why these are outstanding. Or take obscure names out of the *Guinness Book of Records*, and get students to find out what record they hold by asking questions.

BOX 14a

> **Comparative quiz**
> 1 Where are there more people: in Indonesia or Japan?
> 2 Which is the larger country: the USSR or China?
> 3 Which can live longer: a man or an elephant?
> 4 Which is the smaller country: the Vatican or Nauru (island in the Pacific)?
> 5 Which can jump farther: a kangaroo or a horse?
> 6 Which country produces more rice: China or India?
> 7 Which is bigger: a Boeing 747 or a DC 10?
> 8 Which ocean is deeper: the Atlantic or the Pacific?

© Cambridge University Press 1988

Answers

1 Japan	2 the USSR	3 a man	4 Nauru	5 a kangaroo
6 China	7 a Boeing 747	8 the Pacific		

BOX 14b

Superlative quiz

1 Which is the highest mountain in Africa?
2 Which is the largest planet (in the solar system)?
3 Which animal lives the longest?
4 Which is the largest snake in the world?
5 Which country produces the most wheat?
6 Which language has the most words?
7 Which is the lowest place in the world?
8 Which is the fastest animal in the world?

© Cambridge University Press 1988

Answers

1 Kilimanjaro   2 Jupiter   3 the turtle   4 the anaconda
5 the USSR   6 English   7 the Dead Sea
8 the cheetah

6 Conditional clauses

(Note: in this section, the term *first conditional* refers to the construction as in the sentence *If I come, I will see him*; the *second conditional* to *If I came, I would see him*, and the *third conditional* to *If I had come, I would have seen him*.)

6.1 Finishing conditional sentences (1)

First or second conditional sentences; slight variations of controlled patterns; oral brainstorming.

Procedure: Give a sentence using the first conditional, describing one of a number of possible variations, preferably based on personal taste. For example:
>   If I go to France this summer I will visit ... the Eiffel Tower.
>   If I had a million dollars I would buy ... a luxury yacht.

(More examples in *Box 15*) Invite students to express their own variations.
>   If I go to France this summer, I will visit the Eiffel Tower.
>   If I go to France this summer, I will visit the Louvre.
>   If I go to France this summer, I will visit the Opera.

This may be done fairly briskly, going round the class; or each student may be required to write down his or her variation.

Variations: Each student composes his or her own variation and then goes round trying to find someone else with the same. If the activity is done in full class, students may later try to recall what other students' variations were:
>   If Mario goes to France, he will visit the Louvre.

⟫→

BOX 15

Finishing conditional sentences (1)

1 If I go to France this summer, I will visit ...
2 If I feel very hungry this evening, I will eat ...
3 If I have time next weekend, I will go to ...
4 If I have to write a story for homework, I will write about ...
5 If you come to my home, you will see ...

6 If I had a million dollars, I would buy ...
7 If you asked me out for a meal, I would order ...
8 If I could live anywhere I wanted, I would live ...
9 If I had 20 children, I would be ...
10 If I had a museum, I would collect ...

© Cambridge University Press 1988

6.2 Finishing conditional sentences (2)

First or second conditional; variations of set patterns, less controlled than (6.1) above; oral, with optional written follow-up.

Procedure: Give students only the *if* clause of a conditional sentence:
    If I go away on holiday this year ...
and invite them to compose their own endings (see *Box 16* for more examples of half-sentences).
Variations: Give the 'result' half of the conditional sentence as a cue:
    I would be rather disappointed if ...
and do the same (more examples in *Box 16*). After hearing a few suggestions, ask students to recall:
    What were the most interesting endings you heard?
    Who remembers what Monique would do?
For homework, another similar half-sentence may be given (not the same one the students have already explored in class!), and students write four or five possible completions, or a complete paragraph enlarging on one particular response.
Comment: Note that it can be very confusing to mix the first and second conditionals in a single activity. Stick to one or the other until you are really sure your students are clear about the differences between them.

BOX 16

Finishing conditional sentences (2)

First conditional

1 If I go away on holiday this year ...
2 If I lose all my money ...
3 If we get too much homework ...
4 If my friend gets into trouble ...
5 If we finish early today ...

6 I'll eat my hat if ...
7 This school will have to close if ...
8 We will all be very happy if ...
9 I will be rather disappointed if ...
10 Will you help me if ... ?

Second conditional

1 If I were a millionaire ...
2 If you loved me ...
3 If I went to live in another country ...
4 If we were all geniuses ...
5 If you came to visit me ...

6 I would stand on my head if ...
7 We would all be very ill if ...
8 Our teacher would be delighted if ...
9 Would you be well prepared if ...?
10 My friend would give me a kiss if ...

© Cambridge University Press 1988

6.3 Chains of events

Use of conditional (any type) to describe results of actions; transformations and some free composition; oral or written.

Procedure: Give the class one *if* clause, similar to those suggested for
   the previous activity:
   > If I had a million dollars ...
   (See *Box 16* for further examples.) One student suggests a possible
result:
   > If I had a million dollars I would buy a yacht.
The next student takes the result, re·forms it into a condition and
suggests a further result; and so on. For example:
   A: If I had a million dollars, I would buy a yacht.
   B: If I bought a yacht, I would go for a sail.
   C: If I went for a sail, there would be a storm.
   D: If there were a storm, my yacht would sink.
The same can be done, of course, using other types of conditional:
   A: If I am ill tomorrow, I shall stay at home.
   B: If I stay at home, I shall miss lessons.
or:
   A: If the car had been going faster, it wouldn't have been able to
      stop in time.
   B: If it hadn't stopped in time, it would have hit the child.
Supply new vocabulary as needed.
Variations: The same can be done in small groups. In writing, it is best
   done as a class activity rather than as homework: each student gets a
   sheet of paper, at the top of which he or she copies down the given
   condition (or each student may be given a different condition, or –
   better – invent their own). The student then fills in a possible result, and
   passes the paper to a neighbour, who thinks of and writes down the
   next event in the chain (using full conditional sentences as in the
   example given for oral work above), and passes it on. After about ten
   minutes there will be a number of 'chains' ready to be read aloud or put
   up on the wall.

6.4 Superstitions

Use of first conditional to describe superstitions; free composition of
single sentences, oral or written.

Procedure: Suggest some well-known superstitions, defining them
   through conditional sentences:
   > If you walk under a ladder you will have bad luck.

If a girl catches the bride's bouquet after a wedding she will be the next to marry.

(Some more suggestions in *Box 17*; see also BIBLIOGRAPHY, under *Other sources.*)

Students are then invited to suggest further superstitions they know, which may be written on the board, or copied down. They will probably need some new vocabulary; supply as needed.

Variations: The class might make a list of as many superstitions as they can, write them out on a big piece of paper and put them on the wall. A lesson or two later, students can be asked to look at the list and try to memorize them. Then the paper is taken down, and in pairs or small groups they try to recall and write down as many as they can.

Comment: Students might find it a little difficult at first to recall superstitions, though they probably know many if reminded. You may need to jog their memories ('What about the one about black cats?'). It is also a good idea to ask them to think of superstitions they know for homework the night before, writing them out in the conditional form, or even simply making brief notes which can be expanded in class.

This activity is particularly interesting with a multilingual group: members can contribute superstitions new to others in the class from their different countries or cultural backgrounds.

BOX 17

Superstitions

1 If you walk under a ladder you will have bad luck.
2 If a girl catches the bride's bouquet after a wedding she will be the next to marry.
3 If you break a mirror you will have seven years' bad luck.
4 If you talk of the Devil he will appear.
5 If you see a small spider you will get a lot of money.
6 If a witch points at you, you will die.
7 If you scratch your left hand you will give money away.
8 If you touch wood your good luck will continue.
9 If you hear an owl in the night a friend will die.
10 If a black cat crosses your path you will have good luck.

6.5 If only

Use of second conditional to express unfulfilled desires; (also, possibly *I wish...* construction); free composition of sentences; mostly written.

Procedure: Tell the students that they are to be given three wishes, and should write down what these would be. This may be done using the *I wish* form, if it has been learnt, or simply *To...* For example:

I wish I were very rich.

I wish I were good at sports.

I wish I could speak English well.

or:

To be rich.

To be good at sports.

To speak English well.

They should then writen down at least one reason **why** they want these things, using the *second conditional*. For example:

If I were very rich, I wouldn't need to work.

If I were good at sports, I would take more exercise.

If I spoke English well, I would be able to travel more.

Check, as far as you can, that their sentences are correct; then ask them to get together in pairs or small groups and share their wishes and reasons.

Variations: If a similar task is given later for written homework, it is a good idea to ask students to suggest more than one reason for each wish, and to discuss its implications more fully.

An amusing variation is to ask students to write down three **negative** wishes – things they would hate to do, or hate to happen to them, possibly using the formula *I would hate it if...*:

I would hate it if I lived at the North Pole.

or again the *To...* form:

To live at the North Pole.

Then the procedure follows that described above.

6.6 Justifying actions

Use of second conditional sentences to describe hypothetical situations; written and spoken responses.

Procedure: Suggest a set of four or five unusual or immoral actions (written on board, or dictated), and ask students to think of justifications for doing them. For example:

Why might you

... jump out of the window?

... steal something?
... deliberately break a glass?
(More examples in *Box 18*.) Students try to think of situations in which they might, perfectly morally and reasonably, perform these actions, and write them down. For example:

If the classroom suddenly caught fire, and if I could not get to the door, I would jump out of the window.

If someone stole something from me, and I knew it but had no way of proving it, I would steal it back.

Note that the descriptions do not have to use the exact words of the initial cue. After a limited time – during which you too write down your own suggestions! – participants share ideas. They should try to make do with vocabulary they know, without asking you for new words.

Variations: Small-group discussions may be held on the basis of students' suggestions in order to decide on the most convincing possible reason (the *if* clause) for each course of action (the 'result' clause). Groups then compare their results with each other, and possibly decide together on the 'best' answers.

The cues may be used as the basis for creative writing, but in this case, students should be encouraged to describe more details, or to add further suggestions as to circumstances which would justify the action.

BOX 18

```
Why might you ...

1 ... jump out of the window?
2 ... steal money?
3 ... deliberately break a glass?
4 ... pretend to be someone else?
5 ... take off all your clothes in a public place?
6 ... drive a car on the wrong side of the road?
7 ... jump off the top of a cliff?
8 ... set fire to your house?
9 ... cheat in an exam?
10 ... paint yourself green?
```

© Cambridge University Press 1988

6.7 Looking back

Use of third conditional to describe contrary-to-fact past situations; written work as basis for discussion.

Procedure: Students are told to write down three things they have done (or not done) in their lives which, in retrospect, they regret; and three things they are glad they did. This may be written down as follows:

> *Things I regret*
> I didn't go to University.
> I never knew my grandmother.
> I quarrelled with a good friend.
> *Things I am glad about*
> I had children young.
> I came here to study English.
> I was one of a big family.

They are then told to imagine what it might have meant to them if these things had not occurred, and write down sentences expressing what *would have* happened had things been different. Supply new vocabulary to individuals as needed.

> If I had gone to University, I would have got a better job.
> If I had known my grandmother, I would have been able to hear about her experiences.
> If I hadn't had children young, I wouldn't have been free to learn a new profession at the age of 40.
> If I hadn't come here to learn English, I'd have missed making some great friends.

Afterwards, students share and discuss experiences in small groups. Each participant in turn chooses one item to talk about. Other participants should be encouraged to react and comment on what is said, particularly if they have had similar – or conflicting – experiences.

Variations: For writing, an essay title can be given such as *Why I regret . . .* or *Why I am glad I . . .* You may wish to direct students to use conditional sentences in their essays; but these would be likely to occur anyway, particularly if the essay is given as a follow-up to the classroom activity described above.

Comment: Some students find it difficult to think of ideas, others have plenty: so let the more inventive ones think of as many as they like, while others may only have one or two.

This activity is most appropriate for adult learners.

See also:

7 'Copula' verbs

(Verbs whose complements refer back to the subject, e.g. 'Jane looks happy.')

7.1 Defining by sense

Verbs of sensing + adjective; free composition of simple sentences based on object cue; written and oral.

Procedure: Describe an object to the class, through as many senses as you can, and ask the class to guess what the object is. For example:

It feels smooth and hard.
It tastes sweet or sometimes a bit acid.
It looks attractive.
It smells slightly sweet.

– the answer being 'an apple'. Then invite them, in pairs or groups to invent similar definitions for other objects for you and the rest of the class to guess. Some ideas for objects which lend themselves to such definitions are given in *Box 19*.

Variations: For homework, ask students to write you similar definitions for three objects of their choice, which you then have to guess.

BOX 19

> **How do they look/sound/smell/feel/taste?**
>
> 1 an apple 2 a baby 3 chicken soup 4 a parrot
>
> 5 a fur coat 6 a violin 7 an orange tree 8 a hand grenade

© Cambridge University Press 1988

7.2 Not what it seems

Use of 'copula' verbs to contrast what something seems like with what it is; written and oral.

Procedure: Give students the second half of a sentence, beginning 'but in fact...', for example:
... but in fact it's very good for you.
... but in fact he is wicked.
and ask them to reconstruct a possible first half:

It doesn't taste very nice ...
He looks friendly ...

and decide what the sentence refers to (for example, 'bran', or an evil character in a film). There are some examples of cue half-sentences in *Box 20a*. See how many variations (and how many subjects) you can find for each cue.

Variations: When they are used to this sentence-form, students can be given only names of items referred to (*Box 20b*), and make up the full sentences themselves (possibly for homework).

Comment: Apart from 'sensing' verbs (taste, feel, smell, etc.), you may like to add *seem* and *appear*, and allow the possibility of using ... *like* ('It smells like a lemon...') as well as the adjective ('He seems happy...').

BOX 20a

> **Not what they seem (1)**
>
> 1 ... but in fact it's very good for you.
> 2 ... but in fact he's rather nice.
> 3 ... but in fact it's very enjoyable.
> 4 ... but in fact they are poisonous.
> 5 ... but in fact it's quite safe.
> 6 ... but in fact she's very gentle.
> 7 ... but in fact it's no good at all.
> 8 ... but in fact they work very well.

© Cambridge University Press 1988

BOX 20b

> ### Not what they seem (2)
>
> 1 Superman   2 a wise old woman
> 3 a confidence trickster   4 guavas   5 vitamin pills
> 6 Snow White's poisoned apple   7 an old book
> 8 a broken radio   9 an ageing actor

© Cambridge University Press 1988

8 Countable/uncountable, singular/plural nouns

8.1 Remembering pairs

('Pelmanism', 'Memory game'.) Insertion of *a/an/some*, use of singular/plural forms; short oral responses to picture cues.

Materials: Sets of small cards made up of matched pairs whose link is immediately and easily grasped. For example, pairs of pictures of identical objects; or of the same objects in singular and plural; or pictures and corresponding words or phrases (any of these sets may be derived from the material given in *Box 21*). One set should consist of about 40 items (20 pairs). Published sets of small picture cards for language learning can be used to make materials for this activity (see BIBLIOGRAPHY).

Procedure: Students work in pairs or threes, with the cards randomly distributed before them, face down. The first student turns over any two cards and reads the written text(s) or defines the picture(s):

     an umbrella
     some sheep
     a boy

then replaces them face down. This process is repeated, in turn, by the participants, the aim being to remember where the different cards were located and to turn up a matching pair – which then becomes the property of the one who found them. The winner is the one who has the most pairs at the end.

BOX 21

Pairs for remembering

| a cat | | (some) cats |

BOX 21   continued

an orange		(some) oranges	
a man		(some) men	
a child		(some) children	
a woman		(some) women	
a foot		(some) feet	
an elephant		(some) elephants	
a sheep		(some) sheep	

BOX 21 continued

an aeroplane		(some) aeroplanes	
a house		(some) houses	
(some) milk		(some) wood	
(some) grass		(some) paper	
(some) fruit		(some) glass	
(some) snow		(some) money	
(some) clothes		(some) people	

© Cambridge University Press 1988

8.2 Piling up stores

Insertion of *a/an/some* before appropriate nouns, use of singular/plural forms; brief oral responses based on given pattern; optional written follow-up.

Procedure: You start off with a sentence such as:
> In my kitchen store I have a carrot.

The first student continues:
> In my kitchen store I have a carrot and some sugar.

The second:
> In my kitchen store I have a carrot, some sugar and some eggs.

And so on, each student adding another item until the sentence becomes impossible to remember, or until you decide the class has had enough.

Variations: The introductory sentence given above is quite arbitrary; it is probably better to invent your own, based on some local place or circumstance.

Immediately you have finished one such 'round', ask students to see if they can recall, in writing, all the items mentioned – and see if you can yourself. Then check each other.

I usually use food as the topic, because it provides plenty of varied examples of countable and uncountable nouns. But there is no reason why you should not 'pile up' classroom equipment, clothing, or any miscellaneous collection of items you like.

8.3 Kim's game

Insertion of *a/an/some* before appropriate nouns; use of singular/plural forms; brief, mainly written responses; follow-up discussion, using *how much/how many*.

Materials: A tray displaying about 20 different items, which can be defined by a variety of singular and plural nouns, all known to the students.

Procedure: Let the students look at the items for a minute or two, then cover the tray with a cloth to hide it. Ask them to recall and write down as many of the objects as they can – with appropriate determiners, of course. Then check answers, and see who is the 'champion'.

Variations: If the items are distributed in varying quantities ('a litre of milk', 'six stones'), then you might ask them to recall exactly *how much/many* of each there was. In groups, each student recalls and notes down all the quantities he or she can remember, and then asks other group members:
> How much/many X was there?

in order to complete the list.

8.4 Equipment for a project

Insertion of *a/an/some* before appropriate nouns; use of singular/plural forms; also *how much/how many*; short written phrases, with discussion follow-up.

Procedure: Give the class a project which they have to plan, such as a meal, a camping expedition, a class outing, a party, a weekend course, a propaganda campaign. It may be an imaginary one, or some real event which is actually planned for the near future. Discuss with them what equipment they will need for it, listing three or four items they suggest, with appropriate determiner (*a, an* or *some*), on the board. Then ask them to finish the list in small groups, helping with new vocabulary as necessary. Next, working with the full class, compile a definitive list on the board, agreed on by all. Finally, decide – in groups or all together – *how much/many* of each item will be necessary.

Variations: It is a good idea to compile your own list of equipment in advance; this may be then presented as a possible 'right' answer, to which they can compare their own – or simply as a source of more ideas.

8.5 Shopping

Insertion of *a/an/some/any* before apropriate nouns, use of singular/plural forms; oral dialogue.

Materials: Individual copies of lists of about 40 simple items. These may be written out with *a/an/some*, or without: it depends how far you feel your students can be relied on to produce the correct determiners on their own. Also, at least two pictures of each item on separate cards or pieces of paper (80 pictures). A sample list is in *Box 22*; corresponding pictures can be found in *Box 5*, page 56.

Procedure: Half the students divide the pictures randomly between them: they are the sellers. The others, the buyers, take the written lists, and each chooses ten items he or she wishes to buy. They then approach the sellers, who do **not** openly display their wares, and request their items.

Do you have any apples?

Yes, here you are. / No, I'm sorry, I don't have any.

After four or five minutes, see who has managed to buy – or sell – most items. Then the buyers and sellers change over, and pictures and lists are redistributed.

Comment: This activity works best with younger learners, and beginners

For the latter, it is a good idea to provide a set dialogue (as quoted above, for example), and individual five- or ten-item shopping lists.

There is a lot of material to be prepared for this activity; but it can be reused, and I have found the work put into it a good investment. Published sets of picture cards for language learning (see BIBLIOGRAPHY) can be used.

BOX 22

Shopping

1 (some) carrots	15 (some) potatoes	29 (some) bananas
2 (a) book	16 (a) pen	30 (an) apple
3 (a) hat	17 (a) coat	31 (a) shirt
4 (an) umbrella	18 (a) watch	32 (a) handbag
5 (some) coffee	19 (some) milk	33 (some) sugar
6 (an) electric fire	20 (a) chair	34 (a) table
7 (some) flowers	21 (some) wine	35 (a) cake
8 (a) radio	22 (a) television	36 (some) rice
9 (some) glasses	23 (some) meat	37 (some) plates
10 (some) matches	24 (some) eggs	38 (some) bread
11 (some) wine	25 (a) pair of shoes	39 (a) scarf
12 (a) penknife	26 (some) butter	40 (some) money
13 (some) tea	27 (a) bicycle	42 (some) gloves
14 (a) vase	28 (some) trousers	41 (a) watch

© Cambridge University Press 1988

8.6 Shopping list

Use of *a/an/some* (and possibly *any*) with appropriate nouns; use of singular/plural forms: oral dialogue.

Materials: Individual copies of one shopping list, consisting of nouns known to the students, preceded by *a/an/some*, or with no determiners at all (depending on how well your students can be relied on to produce the correct determiners on their own). Examples in *Box 23a.*

Procedure: Tell the students that each should choose five items from the list which they would like to buy. But products can only be supplied if

Activities

there is sufficient demand: so in order to 'buy' an item, each student has to find at least four others who want it. Working in 'fluid pairs', they try to find 'co-buyers':

I want some ... and a ..., do you?

I want some ... too, but I don't want a ...

A time limit of four or five minutes for this should be plenty. Afterwards they report back how many items they have succeeded in 'buying' (i.e. have found four 'co-buyers' for).

Variations: The same procedure can be repeated immediately afterwards, with students trying to get a higher 'score' of successful 'buys'.

The things to be bought do not have to be real marketable commodities; students may enjoy doing this activity on the basis of a list of more imaginative 'desirables' – an extra ten years of life, for example, or a perfect figure (see *Box 23b*).

Comment: You may find that you have to make the number of 'co-buyers' larger or smaller, according to the size of your class.

BOX 23a

Shopping list

List A

1 (a) colour television
2 (a) motorboat
3 (some) land (for farming)
4 (a) fast car
5 (an) electric typewriter
6 (a) country cottage
7 (some) kitchen equipment
8 (some) courses of study
9 (some) gold
10 (some) good food
11 (an) apartment
12 (some) tickets for a holiday cruise
13 (some) theatre tickets
14 (some) clothes for my holiday
15 (some) improvements to my home
16 (some) furniture

© Cambridge University Press 1988

BOX 23b

Shopping list

List B

1 (some) fun
2 (an) automatic house–cleaner
3 (some) more time to do things
4 (a) new job
5 (a) trip into the future (of my choice)
6 (some) patience
7 (some) excitement
8 (an) extra ten years of life
9 (some) advice on my problems
10 (some) more friends
11 (some) more progress in English
12 (a) talent for music or art
13 (an) achievement
14 (some) peace and quiet
15 (a) perfect figure

© Cambridge University Press 1988

See also:
4.1 *Association dominoes* (for plural forms);
11.1 *Bingo*, 11.2 *Quick Bingo*, using varied countable and uncountable items;
11.4 *Possessions*;
16.1 *Describing pictures (1)*, 16.2 *Describing pictures (2)*.

9 Future tenses

9.1 What will you do with it?

Use of *going to* or *will* to express planned future action; oral brainstorm.

Materials: A collection of small, readily recognizable, objects in a bag; or a set of picture cards depicting similar objects; or the names of the same items written on slips of paper (see *Box 24*).

Procedure: Display one object or picture to all the class except for one student, who has to guess what it is. The guesser asks:

What will you / are you going to do with it?

and the other members of the class then describe their (imaginary) plans for the object. Their utterances should preferably express less obvious or conventional uses, so that the guessing is made more challenging, and the hints more entertaining. For example, if the article is a cup, students may say things like:

I will / am going to water plants with it.
I will / am going to break it.
I will / am going to make sandcastles with it.

as well as the more conventional:

I will / am going to drink tea from it.

Variations: After a few such objects have been guessed, one can be displayed again, and you ask:

Who remembers what will be done with this object?

If you wish to practise the future passive, answers may take the form:

It will be broken.
It will be painted.

– otherwise they may simply recall who said what:

Simone is going to break it.
Antonio is going to paint flowers on it.

BOX 24

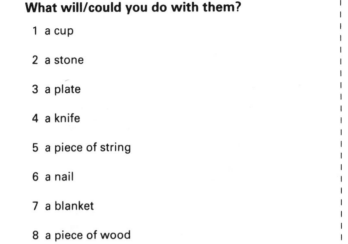

What will/could you do with them?

1 a cup

2 a stone

3 a plate

4 a knife

5 a piece of string

6 a nail

7 a blanket

8 a piece of wood

9 a box of matches

10 a shoebox

11 a sheet of paper

12 a piece of cotton wool

13 a litre of water

14 a lump of clay

9.2 Diaries

Use of *going to* to express future plans; oral or written responses, based on more or less controlled sentence patterns.

Materials: A diary showing the days of the week filled in with notes of different planned activities (*Box 25*). This may be presented on

BOX 25

Diary

	Monday	Tuesday	Wednesday	Thursday	Friday	Saturday	Sunday
	07.30–09.00 get breakfast, send kids to school	07.30–09.00 get breakfast, send kids to school	06.00 get up, go to airport 07.00 fly to London	07.30–09.00 get breakfast, send kids to school	08.30 get up, (Pat sees to kids)	08.30 get up, breakfast	10.00 get up, breakfast
	09.00–11.00 housework, shopping with Pat	09.00–13.00 office	08.00–13.00 get home, housework, shopping, lunch	09.00–11.00 office	09.00–11.00 washing, housework	10.00 take kids to football practice	11.00–13.00 do some gardening, help Pat with lunch
	11.00–13.00 office			11.00–13.00 meeting with Mike	11.00–13.00 office, work on new project	10.30–11.30 meet Kit for coffee 11.30–12.30 watch end of football, take kids home	

13.00–15.00 lunch with Tony, discuss new project 15.00–17.30 office 18.00–19.00 help kids with homework 19.00–20.00 supper 20.00–23.00 watch TV	13.00 lunch 13.30 leave for airport 14.45 fly to Dublin 17.00 meeting with Irish colleagues 19.00–22.00 dinner at Trinity College	13.00–14.00 office 14.00–15.30 discuss Irish trip with boss 15.30–17.30 go home, rest 18.00–23.00 quiet evening with family	13.00–16.00 office, leave free for any new problems 16.30–18.30 tea at Mother's with kids 18.30–19.30 shower, change 20.00–22.00 evening out at Italian restaurant with Pat	13.00–14.30 lunch with boss, discuss new project 14.30–17.00 interview new candidates, next week's schedule 17.00–22.00 supper with Pat's parents	13.00–14.00 lunch 14.00–15.30 rest 15.30–16.30 tennis with Pat, Max, Carol 17.30–18.30 shower, change 19.00–23.30 party at Sylvia and Bob's	13.00–14.00 lunch 14.00–16.00 rest, more gardening 17.30 tea, take kids to youth group 18.00–23.00 lazy evening: write letters watch TV

individual worksheets, or on acetate film to be shown on an overhead
projector.

Procedure: Using the diary as in *Box 25* students expand the notes in
the squares to full sentences. They may use the first person, or, if the
diary is assigned to an individual (called, say, Mickey), the third. For
example, the note 'office' at 9 a.m. on Thursday becomes:

I am going to be in the office from nine a.m. on Thursday.
or:

Mickey is going to be in the office...

This may be done orally, round the class, or in writing. If the latter,
students may be asked to expand all the entries for one day into full
sentences (a bit tedious), or select for writing only a set number of
activities according to some subjective criterion: those they think they
will enjoy, for example, or those they think they are likely to forget,
and therefore need to write in full.

Variations: After the students have worked for a while on one such
grid, it may be taken in and a blank one (*Box 26*) shown on the
overhead projector or drawn on the board. Students then have to try
and fill it in from memory: one student, for example, might recall:

I am going to be in the office from nine a.m. on Thursday.

whereupon you, or a volunteer student, fill in the note 'office' in the
appropriate space. The same may be done in groups: each group gets a
blank grid, and one 'secretary' fills in everything members of the group
can remember – taking care to accept only full future-tense sentences!

⟫→ *p. 100*

9.3   Finding a time to meet

Use of present progressive or *going to* to express future plans; oral questions and answers.

Procedure: In pairs, each student has a different schedule for a week (*Box 27*, for example). They have to try to find at least one time when both are free to meet (or, preferably two or three possible times, out of which they choose the most convenient). They do this by asking each other questions:

>   What are you doing / going to do on Tuesday?
>   Are you going to be free at seven on Friday?

If they cannot meet their partner at the time proposed, they must say why (i.e. describe what they *are going to do / are doing* then). After a few minutes, check to see whether all pairs have found one or more of the 'correct' times to meet.

Variations: Give students blank grids (as in *Box 26*) and tell them to fill about two thirds or three quarters of it with their own imaginary – or genuine! – programme of activities for the coming week. They then talk to partners and try to find times they are both free to meet. As an optional continuation, they may go on to try to fix a further appointment with someone else – and so on, until the diary is full, or until they are unable to find anyone to meet in the little spare time remaining.

⋙→ *p. 102–5*

BOX 26

Blank diary

	Monday	Tuesday	Wednesday	Thursday	Friday	Saturday	Sunday
07.00–09.00							
09.00–11.00							
11.00–13.00							
13.00–15.00							

15.00–17.00			
17.00–19.00			
19.00–21.00			
21.00–23.00			

Activities

BOX 27a

A student's diary

Student A

	Monday	Tuesday	Wednesday	Thursday	Friday	Saturday	Sunday
07.00–09.00	get up, breakfast	get up, breakfast	get up, breakfast	get up, breakfast	get up, breakfast	sleep	sleep
09.00–11.00	English lesson	shopping		French lesson	philosophy lecture	get up, breakfast	sleep
11.00–13.00	French literature lecture		English literature lecture	meet tutor		basketball practice	get up, breakfast
13.00–15.00	lunch; student union meeting		lunch; read in library		lunch; shopping		5-mile run; lunch

15.00–17.00	basketball practice	linguistics seminar		basketball practice	philosophy seminar	tea with tutor	
17.00–19.00	work on assign-ments	read in library	read in library		work on assign-ments	work on assign-ments	
19.00–21.00		supper; work on assign-ments	supper; go to cinema	supper; read in library	party	supper, read	
21.00–23.00	sports club meeting	early night	cinema	write letters		party	pub with friends

BOX 27b

A student's diary

Student B

	Monday	Tuesday	Wednesday	Thursday	Friday	Saturday	Sunday
07.00–09.00	get up, breakfast	get up, breakfast	get up, breakfast	get up, breakfast	get up, breakfast	get up, breakfast	get up, breakfast
09.00–11.00		biology lab	chemistry lab		biology lecture	swim	
11.00–13.00		biology lab	chemistry lab	philosophy of science seminar		work in library	swim
13.00–15.00	lunch; shopping	lunch; computer practice		lunch; computer practice	lunch; shopping	lunch; walk in country	

15.00–17.00	biology lab	computer practice	chemistry lecture	computer practice	work in library	walk in country	
17.00–19.00	swim	swim		swim	swim		visit family
19.00–21.00		supper; work in library	supper; work in library		theatre	visit family	
21.00–23.00	early night		work in library	party		theatre	visit family

9.4 Future of a picture

Use of *going to* or *about to* to describe imminent action; oral brain-storming; optional written follow-up.

Materials: A picture of some kind of interesting or dramatic action, displayed to the class or distributed to individual participants. Examples in *Box 28*; or use cut-out magazine pictures.

Procedure: Ask the class 'What do you think will / is going to happen next?', and students contribute suggestions, using the specified future form. They may be asked to give evidence for their ideas, or try to decide which of the suggestions is the most likely. Give new vocabulary as needed.

Variations: Usually this activity takes the form of a free brainstorm; but sometimes there may be a 'right' answer – if, for example, the picture is taken from a play or film and you know what comes next; or if the picture is one of a series (e.g. one of those in *Box 59*, page 216), with the sequel available. Then the activity may take the form of a guessing-game, and you can help with hints ('Look carefully at that character in the corner and think again!' ... 'You're very close!').

For homework, several such pictures may be given and the students write a sentence for each; or one picture may serve as stimulus for a full paragraph.

BOX 28

Pictures with a future

BOX 28 continued

2

3

⟫→

BOX 28   continued

4

5

BOX 28   continued

6

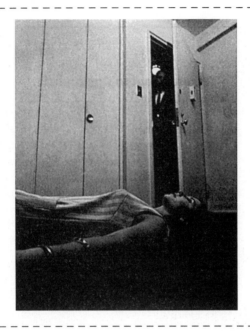

9.5   Mime continuation

Use of interrogative of *going to* or *about to* to ask about imminent action;
free oral responses based on mime cues.

Materials: A set of cue-cards or slips of paper, on each one of which is
   written a sentence using *going to* or *about to*, describing an action
   about to be done. For example:
   You are going to drive a car.
   (Further ideas in *Box 29.*)

Procedure: One student takes a slip, and mimes things he or she might
   do leading up to the (future) action. The others have to guess what is
   about to happen, using question forms, and trying to get as near as
   possible to the text of the cue-card.
   Are you going to / about to drive a car?
   The mime should not, of course, include a demonstration of the action
   itself.

Variations: Students may invent their own 'future actions' to mime. If this is done, you should have a reserve supply of ideas ready to help the less imaginative or confident ones.

BOX 29

You are about to / going to ...

1 You are going to drive a car.

2 You are going to wash your face.

3 You are going to drink a cup of tea.

4 You are going to swim.

5 You are going to play a guitar.

6 You are going to shout.

7 You are going to fall asleep.

8 You are going to work.

9 You are going to pick a flower.

BOX 29 continued

10 You are going to play cricket.

11 You are going to paint a picture.

12 You are going to dance.

© Cambridge University Press 1988

9.6 Future of an object

Use of *going to* or *will*, especially in the passive, to describe non-imminent future events; group oral brainstorming, free discussion.

Procedure: Suggest a simple object or raw material – an egg, for example – and ask students what they think *will / is going to* happen to it in the future. For instance:

It will be part of a cake.
It will fall on the floor and break.

Then give groups of students lists of five or six such items (ideas in *Box 30*) and ask them to note down possible future 'destinies' for each one – as many as they can think of within the vocabulary they know. Ideas are noted down by a 'secretary'. Later all the groups' ideas for each item are compared or pooled: which object/material is the most versatile?

Variations: The group is asked to list all the things that will be done to the object in a possible sequence. The egg, for example:

will be sold, will be put in a fridge, will be taken out, will be broken, will be fried, etc.

⋙→

111

BOX 30

Objects with a future

1 a stone	2 a potato	3 a plank of wood
4 a lump of wood	5 a screw	6 a battery
7 a bar of iron	8 a sheet of glass	9 an egg
10 a spring	11 a bag of sugar	12 a litre of water
13 an orange	14 a diamond	15 a roll of paper
16 a plastic bag	17 grapes	18 a microchip

BOX 30   continued

19 some steel wire	20 a cardboard box	21 a chain
22 a bottle	23 a carton of milk	24 four tyres

© Cambridge University Press 1988

9.7   Plans for a trip

Use of *going to* or *will* to express future plans; free discussion or writing, some reading.

Materials: A collection of data about places and/or things to do on a trip or holiday. This might consist of a list of possible activities (*Box 31a*); a list of equipment or gear that will be needed (*Box 31b*); part of a holiday brochure (*Box 31c*); or a map of an area to be toured with places of interest marked (*Box 31d*). Each student should have a copy of the data you have chosen to work on.

Procedure: Tell the students that they have a week off for a trip, and they have to draw up an itinerary and programme of activities, bringing in all (or as much as possible of) the data they have been given, and using the prescribed future form. After one such exercise done with all the class together, they may do a similar task in groups, pairs or individually. They should write out the finished plan in complete sentences and paragraphs. Different programmes can later be read out and compared.

Variations: Each participant tells the others, or writes down, one thing that he or she would really like to do on holiday. Then the programme has to include something for everyone.

A programme based on the limitation of a sum of money may be made into a group competition. Tell the students that there is a sum of a thousand/three thousand/ten thousand pounds available to be won for a trip abroad: the group with the best plan for a trip using this money will get it. The judge may be you or (better) a panel of students, who work out what their main criteria will be for judging entries while the others are planning their trips.

You may wish to ask your class to write out their plans neatly and add maps and illustrations for displaying on the classroom wall.

Comment: This activity is basically a simulation, and the more seriously the students relate to it the better. Keep them aware of real-life factors, and remind them to make their programmes realistic and practical ('That's a nice schedule, but have you considered what you'll do if it rains?' . . . 'Don't you think that's a bit tiring, all in one day?'). If the plan can be linked to a real trip due to take place in the near future, so much the better.

Note that the more explicit the preliminary data, the easier and more controlled the exercise: the list of activities (*Box 31a*) virtually dictates the content of most of the sentences of the plan, the list of equipment/accessories and the brochure (*Boxes 31b* and *31c*) allow more room for variation, though giving some lexis on which to base sentences, and the use of the map (*Box 31d*) makes the students invent their own sentences more or less from scratch.

BOX 31a

Holiday activities

> Skiing, skating, dancing, sunbathing, eating out, walking, resting, meeting people, touring.

> Swimming, scuba-diving, visiting nightclubs, walking, sunbathing, sailing, driving, seeing shows, fishing.

> Camping, walking, cycling, riding, swimming, visiting stately homes, learning about nature, rock-climbing.

> Resting, taking hot baths, sunbathing, reading, seeing films, hearing interesting talks, listening to music, eating good food, coach-touring.

© Cambridge University Press 1988

BOX 31b

Holiday gear and equipment

Passport, air ticket, swimming costume, skis, skates, sunglasses, guide book, suntan oil, evening clothes, strong shoes.

Goggles and snorkel, bathing costume, harpoon, fishing-rod, evening clothes, life jacket, driving licence, camera.

Tent, sleeping bag, strong shoes, bicycle, riding clothes, guide books, books on plants and animals, nylon rope, swimming costume, hat, sunglasses, torch.

© Cambridge University Press 1988

BOX 31c

Holiday brochure

The Channel Islands

Jersey

The largest of the group, Jersey lies 100 miles from Weymouth on England's south coast. Despite its small area – about 45 square miles – there are some 500 miles of roads suitable for motoring and it's easy to hire a car. The scenery varies from magnificent cliffs on the north coast to sandy beaches on the south, with lush valleys in between.

St Helier is Jersey's capital, and has plenty of shops and entertainment in its charming narrow streets. See 16th-century Elizabeth Castle in St Aubin's Bay, reached by a narrow causeway or by ferry at high tide. Near the village of Gorey you'll find Mont Orgueil Castle with its tableaux and museum, while the village itself boasts a pottery centre where you can see craftsmen at work.

Sporting enthusiasts are well catered for – golf, motor-racing, surfing and underwater swimming are among the many pursuits you can follow – or simply relax on one of the clean, golden beaches hiding among rocky headlands.

BOX 31c continued

Winter in Britain

This is the season for visits to the theatre, opera, concerts and ballet, or for discovering the treasures of the hundreds of museums and galleries throughout the country. Soccer is in full swing and there's rugby, too, with thrilling international matches at the famous grounds of Twickenham in London, Cardiff Arms Park in Wales and Murrayfield in Scotland. If you prefer four-legged sport, it's the steeplechase season, with meetings at major racecourses in all areas of Britain. If you're energetic and like to take part in sports, Scotland is the place for you at this time of year, as centres such as Aviemore have excellent facilities for winter sports and year-round holiday entertainment.

If you prefer a more relaxed way of life, you can eat out by cosy candlelight, or have a few drinks beside a roaring log fire in a country pub.

London's attractions

London has plenty to offer during the winter months, especially in the way of entertainment – and the shops act like a magnet with their array of presents for the Christmas shopper, followed by bargains galore in the January sales. But it's not only London that offers value shopping – most of our suburban and provincial centres have just as much to offer the eager shopper.

Even if you're based in London, you don't have to spend all your time there – and that goes for all the year round, too. Take a train or coach and see what else Britain has to offer; there are many excursions, even in winter, and among the great country houses which keep their stately front doors open throughout the year are Longleat and Woburn Abbey. Hire a car and drive out into the beauty of the winter landscape – the scenery is still beautiful – and the people will have more time to chat to you at this time of year.

BOX 31d

Map of holiday island

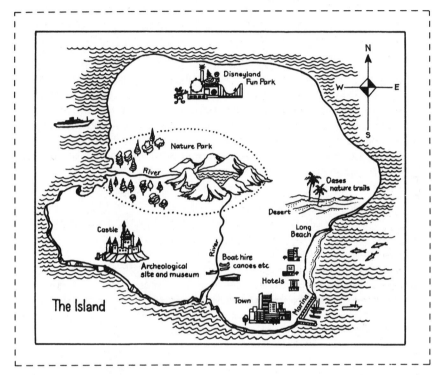

9.8 How will the story end?

Use of *going to* or *will* to describe future events; reading, oral brainstorming or discussion, with optional written follow-up.

Materials: A story, presented initially to the students without its ending, or with an uncertain or ambivalent ending. Such stories are most conveniently given as individual written copies, but may also be read aloud or improvised orally from skeleton notes. They may be taken from the coursebook or from books of stories and anecdotes (see BIBLIOGRAPHY).

The material may be presented very effectively in the form of a recorded short story, radio play or dramatized narrative, or a (video) film stopped at some point before the denouement.

Procedure: Present the incomplete story, and invite suggestions as to how it will continue. Students may brainstorm simple one-sentence suggestions, or discuss each idea as it is proposed, accepting, rejecting or amending in order to work out an agreed sequence of events. You may disclose the 'right' ending (if there is one) at the end of the activity – or adopt one of their suggestions – or approve them all.

Variations: The activity may be made a little longer and more varied by stopping the story at several different points as it goes on, not just at the end. You may read a long story in instalments, stopping at exciting points to ask the class what they think will happen next (continuing, possibly, in later lessons); or a video film, a recorded narrative or play may be halted occasionally to give opportunities for conjecture.

For homework, students write out their prediction of the sequence of events following an incomplete story.

Comment: The fact that the story is to lead to suggestions for further action in the future tense does not necessarily mean that it has to be told in the present; it is quite acceptable to use the past tense in the narrative and then use the future to discuss possible sequels.

For those who teach literature as part of the English syllabus, this technique can be used when presenting a story, play or novel for the first time to stimulate discussion of plot or character ('Judging from what you know of X's personality, how do you think she will react when she finds out . . . ?', ' . . . Do you think this is going to end happily or tragically?', ' . . . Why?').

9.9 Horoscopes

Use of *going to* or *will* to express non-imminent future events; mainly writing.

Procedure: Ask the students to compose a horoscope for an unknown person on a loose sheet of paper: it should be interesting and not too serious. It may relate to a limited future time (next week/month/year) or to the person's entire future life. Try to get students to base their writing on vocabulary they already know, without getting new words from you. The papers are folded, collected, and placed in a hat, bag or other container. Each member of the class then takes, at random, a piece of paper which is to be 'his or her horoscope' and reads it. Some or all of the 'horoscopes' may be read aloud.

Variations: Ask the students to compose very optimistic and desirable horoscopes. Then, instead of distributing them personally, the horoscopes are put up on the wall round the class. You and the students then go round reading them – and correcting the English, if necessary – and each member of the class chooses one future he or she would like and appends his or her name at the bottom. Students then read out the futures they have chosen for themselves.

Or ask students to compose an ideal horoscope for themselves, and another for someone (anonymous!) they hate; or one for a specific person – you, a fellow-student, a famous politician or television personality.

Comment: For students unfamiliar with the idea of a horoscope, you may need to explain what it is, and possibly show them an example from an English-language newspaper or magazine.

9.10 The world tomorrow

Use of *will* to describe non-imminent future events. Written brainstorm, followed by free discussion.

Procedure: Ask students to write down a list of changes they expect to see in the world by a date 50 years hence. For example:
> We shall have a working day of four hours.
> Every home will have a video telephone.
> People will live to be 100 or more.
> Europe will be a single country.

They may be told to write as many as they can in the time given; or you may want to give them a series of topics (education, technology, politics, fashion, sport, etc.), and ask them to write one or more idea for each; or they may be asked to describe three or four developments they expect to occur in areas they are expert in.

The ideas are then read out and discussed. Those that most of the class agree with may be written up on the board.

Variations: In groups, students can try to sort their predictions into 'optimistic' and 'pessimistic' ones – not always as clear-cut a distinction as you might expect!

Later, students may choose predictions that particularly appeal to them as the topic for a short essay.

See also:
6.1 *Finishing conditional sentences (1)*;
15.5 *Common denominator* (using future in the original sentence);
20.6 *Election campaign* (using active or passive);
20.7 *Results of events* (using active or passive).

10 Future perfect tense

10.1 Kim's diary game

Future perfect tense in simple spoken/written sentences.

Materials: Any of the filled-in diaries in *Boxes 25* and *27*, pages 96, 102 and 104.

Procedure: Ask students a few questions starting 'What will you have done by ... (a certain time on a certain day)', and elicit answers using the future perfect. Then tell them to study two specified days of the week for two or three minutes, and try to memorize the schedule. They then turn the diary-sheets face down, so that they cannot see them, and you ask them to write down what they *will have done* by a specified hour on one of the days – for example, by half past three on Tuesday. They may work individually, or in pairs or groups. Check answers, and see who has remembered most. Then do the same again, with two other days, and see if they can get better scores.

10.2 Predicting achievements

Future perfect tense in simple sentences: oral brainstorming, optional written follow-up.

Procedure: Tell the students to invent for themselves an extremely successful future career in whatever field they like. Give them a minute or two to imagine what kinds of things they will achieve, and to ask you for new vocabulary where needed. They may jot down ideas in writing, and should also note at what age they will have their different successes. Then ask them to tell each other (possibly in groups) what they *will have done* by the age of 30, then by the age of 50, then by the age of 70 (if your students are over 30, adapt ages accordingly). Finally, discuss with them who *will have had* the most successful career of all.

Variations: For homework before the lesson, each student chooses a famous historical personage, and notes down important dates in his or her life. In class, each student gives his or her date of birth, and at least two dates, or ages, by which he or she *will have done* certain things:
It is 1769; my person has just been born.

By 1796 he or she will have married.

By 1806 he or she will have become Emperor.

The other students guess who the personage is. The same can be done in writing for homework, for you to guess.

11 Have/has (got)

(as main verb)

(Note: the verb form *have/has (got)* is arguably only one lexical variation of the present simple or present perfect tense; but it is treated in many textbooks as a separate grammatical item, and therefore I have allotted it a section to itself.

For the sake of simplicity and brevity, I have used only the simpler *have/has* form in my examples; those who teach British English and prefer *have/has got* to express possession will need to amend my sentences accordingly.)

11.1 Bingo

Simple *I have* sentences; controlled oral responses; possibly some simple reading.

Materials: Pictures or written names of objects, animals or people. There should be two copies of each such item: one on a separate piece of card, the other on a sheet showing several items together. The materials cannot be illustrated here as they take up too much space and are too numerous: you can use some children's *Bingo* or *Lotto* games, but I usually adapt sets of picture cards for language learning (see BIBLIOGRAPHY), adding written versions if necessary.

Procedure: Each student has a sheet displaying several items. You (or one of the students acting as 'caller') have the pile of separate cue-cards, and offer each one in random order, using the question 'Who has ... ?'

> Who has a horse?
> Who has the policeman?

The student who possesses the item answers using 'I have':

> I have it / a horse.
> I have him / the policeman.

and receives the card with which he or she covers the item on the sheet. The winner is the first to cover all his or her sheet.

Variations: A useful variation is to lay down the rule that the winner is the one who finishes **last**, so that all items must be called out and claimed, and there is extra practice of the structure.

In order to practise the third person forms, students are put in pairs, each partner having a sheet of cues. A student may not claim for his or her own sheet but only for the partner's, using 'He or she has...'

He or she has it / a horse.

He or she has him / the policeman.

The winners are the pair both of whose sheets are completed first.

11.2 Quick Bingo

Simple *I have* sentences; controlled oral responses; some reading and copying.

Procedure: Give the students duplicated sheets displaying 20 cues, to which the teacher has matching 'partners', and ask each student to cross out any 14 of them, leaving six to work on. Alternatively, each student may get the same 20 cues, but each on a separate small card; they arrange the cards into a 4 × 5 rectangle, in random order. Then the first student to get, say, four items in a straight line is the winner.

Variations: One variation needs no ready-made materials at all. Decide on ten or 12 vocabulary items and write them on the board. Ask each student to copy down any four of them. Then offer the items in random order and the students cross out their corresponding items as they identify them. This is an extremely quick and efficient way of using the *Bingo* technique to practise a small number of specific lexical items, as well as *have/has*.

11.3 Detectives

Affirmative, interrogative and negative of *have*; simple oral repetition.

Procedure: An object to be 'stolen' is decided on – say a coin, or a ring. One student (the 'detective') is sent out of the room. One of the remaining students is given the object: he or she is the 'thief'. The detective returns and tries to find out who is the thief by asking each participant:

Do you have it / the ring?

Each participant – including the actual thief – denies guilt, and accuses someone else:

No, I don't have it, A has it!

Whereupon the detective turns to A with the same question – and so on, until everyone has been asked and has denied responsibility. The detective then has to decide in three guesses who is lying – who 'looks guilty'. The process is then repeated with another detective and another thief.

Variations: The activity may be made more lively by encouraging students to act innocence or indignation as convincingly as they can: they may change the emphasis or intonation of the set sentences as they wish, add gesture and so on. Another technique, which abandons verisimilitude but helps fluency, is to get the class to complete the round of 'interrogation' as quickly as possible: ('Let's see if we can get round the whole class in two minutes' . . . 'Let's see if we can do it again in even less time').

11.4 Possessions

Have/has with first/third person subjects; simple oral responses based on picture cues; possible written follow-up.

Materials: Pictures of small objects, based on vocabulary known to the students, enough for each member of the class to have at least one: those in *Box 5*, page 56, for example, or published pictures for language learning (see BIBLIOGRAPHY).

Procedure: Each student gets a picture. Going round the class, each says what he or she has:

> I have a cat.
> I have some coffee.
> I have a box of matches.

Then students are asked to recall what others have:

> Ahmad has a cat.
> Hasan has some coffee.
> Fayiz has a box of matches.

Variations: Students say not only what they have but also what they don't have – and the latter, of course, is open to the individual student's imagination:

> I have a dog (*shows it*), but I don't have . . . an elephant.
> I have a fish, but I don't have . . . a dolphin.

The recallers then have to remember not only what the other participants have, but also what they do not have – again, using the third person.

In a more personalized version, the pictures are discarded, and students imagine their own items, choosing things they really have that are 'special' for them or that they are proud of. They may add brief comments about their 'possession'. This is a good getting-to-know-you activity for an early stage in the course.

11.5 Happy Families

Questions and answers with *have*; simple oral responses based on set pattern.

Materials: Packs of Happy Family cards, enough for each small group (3–4 students) to have a pack. A pack is composed of eight to ten sets of four cards, each set representing a mother, a father, a son and a daughter in families identified by name and profession (e.g. Mr Bun the Baker, Mrs Bun and so on). However, there are other versions available based on theme-linked sets of objects: a pack based on 'nature', for example, might consist of sets of four flowers, four animals, four birds, four trees, four insects, four fish, four reptiles. It is possible, though time-consuming, to make your own, or get students to make them.

Procedure: Each student gets four random cards, the rest of the pack is placed face down on the table. Each student tries to complete a family; so if one of Student A's cards is Mr Bun the Baker, he or she may turn to any one of the players and ask:

Do you have Mrs Bun the Baker's wife (Miss/Master Bun ...)?
If that player has the card, he or she answers:

Yes, I have him/her,
and gives it to Student A, who can then request another card from any player. If he or she does not have the card, then the answer is:

No, I don't have him/her,
in which case Student A takes the top card of the pack, and the turn passes to the next player. And so on, until all the cards in the pack are gone, and all 'families' are completed. The winner is the player with the most 'families'.

11.6 Had a good day?

Use of *have* with noun to describe action (e.g. *have a shower, have a cup of tea*); mostly writing.

Procedure: Ask the students 'Had a good day yesterday?' and get them to tell you things they did using only phrases with *have*. Put such phrases on the board as they come up, and supplement with some of your own (see *Box 32* for some ideas). Then ask them to describe in writing an imaginary awful day in which everything went wrong – again, they should use phrases with *have*. They can work in groups or pairs, and read out their results, or display them, to the full class. See who can compose the most awful day of all!

Comment: You may want to relax the rules a bit and allow students to use other verbs as well to make the composition more interesting; but limit them: for example, at least half the things they did, or that happened to them, must be expressed in expressions with *have*.

BOX 32

You can have . . .

... things to eat (breakfast, a meal, a snack, a sandwich, a steak)
... things to drink (a cup of tea/coffee, a glass of wine)
... a cigarette
... a rest, a break, a sleep
... a talk, a discussion, a quarrel
... a shower, a bath, a swim
... a game, a run, some exercise
... an outing, a treat, fun
... a good/bad/exciting/dull/happy day or time
... a dream, an idea
... a lesson, a session, a lecture
... a celebration, a party, a picnic
... an operation, an injection, some treatment
... a baby

See also:
8.5 *Shopping*;
16.3 *Picture dictation* (describing a person or animal with plenty of interesting physical features or possessions).

12 Imperatives

12.1 Simon says

Simple commands; understanding and producing short oral utterances.

Procedure: Give the students simple commands:
> Stand up!
> Turn round!

They must obey these commands only if you say 'Simon says' first; if you omit this prefix they should ignore them. Any student who performs a command that was said without 'Simon says' loses a 'life'. They have three lives, after which they are 'out'. Later, students themselves may give the commands.

Variations: Omit the 'Simon says' rule; instead, give a command and at the same time do an action which may or may not correspond to it. The students have to do what you **tell them**, not (necessarily) what they see you do.

Comment: Best for younger students.

12.2 Directions

Use of imperatives to tell someone how to get somewhere; giving and understanding simple oral instructions.

Materials: Individual copies of a road map of a town, as in *Box 33*; you may find similar maps in your coursebook.

Procedure: Review the kinds of commands and other words and formulae needed for requesting and giving directions: in particular, prepositions of place and direction (see list at the end of 25.5 *Where would you like to live?* page 234). Then put students in pairs, with their maps hidden from one another. Student A decides where he or she would like to live (on the map), marks in the site, and instructs Student B how to get there from the Starting Point. Student B then does the same for Student A. They continue to take it in turns to choose what else they will have in 'their' town (a bank, bus station, cinema, etc.), and to direct each other to the site: but they have to go back to the Starting Point every time they give directions. At the end, they compare maps to check their sites correspond; and compare with other pairs to see how many different facilities are boasted by the different towns.

Variations: In writing, ask them to describe a route they know well: from their home to the school, or from the station to the centre of town, etc.

BOX 33

Road map

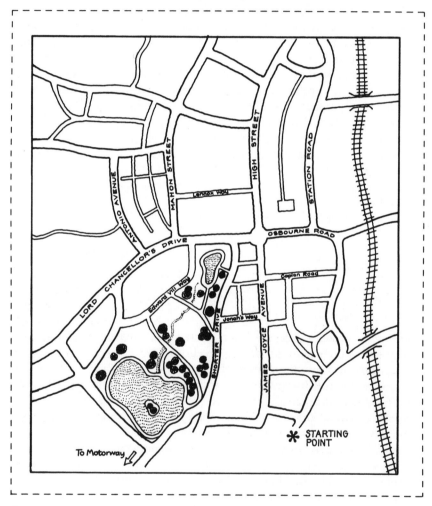

© Cambridge University Press 1988

12.3 Dos and don'ts

Positive and negative commands; written, with oral follow-up, and optional free discussion.

Procedure: Ask each student to think of something he or she is good at; then to think of pieces of advice for someone else new at the job. It could be a sport, a profession, or a hobby. For example, I might write about teaching:

> Learn your students' names as soon as possible.
> Don't talk too much.

Elicit a few examples from students; then ask them all to write at least five positive and five negative pieces of advice; they should try to make do with vocabulary they know, without asking you for more. Then they get together in pairs or groups to advise each other on, or find out about, their different fields of expertise. This may, of course, develop into an informal discussion, and the brief commands may be elaborated, in speech, into more detailed recommendations.

Variations: The same can be done on the basis of advice for a new student or teacher coming into the school or course. In this case, students try to come to a consensus on the best set of 'dos' and 'don'ts' for the purpose.

12.4 Recipes

Use of the imperative to give instructions; fairly free writing.

Procedure: Tell the class to write out instructions for a simple recipe: making a cup of tea, or boiling an egg, for example (more examples in *Box 34*); supply new vocabulary as needed. Then check that all the participants agree as to the best method – or learn alternative methods!

Variations: Ask for a detailed 'recipe' for a very simple operation, like opening a door (second part of *Box 34*): students have to describe everything that has to be done:

> Walk to the door, stop in front of it, turn the handle, push or pull the door open...

When they think they have finished, they exchange papers, and try to find things their partners have forgotten:

> You didn't say: 'put your hand on the handle'.

BOX 34

Give instructions how to ...

1 ... boil an egg
2 ... make a cup of tea
3 ... make a cup of coffee
4 ... make a salad / fruit salad
5 ... make soup
6 ... make scrambled eggs / an omelette

Or how to ...

7 ... open a door
8 ... put on a shirt
9 ... wash your face
10 ... cut a piece of cake
11 ... light a match
12 ... cross the road

12.5 Stances

Simple oral commands to move parts of the body.

Materials: A set of sketches of stick-people in different physical positions, on separate cards or slips of paper (*Box 35*): it is a good idea to have two or three copies of each sketch.

Procedure: Check the students remember names of different parts of the body. Display one card to everybody but one. The students then get that one person to assume the position depicted on the card by giving instructions:

Put your hand on your head ... look to your left...

The same is then done in small groups: each group gets one card, and gives instructions to one of their members. When they have got the latter to take up the position depicted to their satisfaction, the card is exchanged, and another participant is told how to assume another 'stance'.

Variations: This can be done using pictures of models cut from fashion magazines. The 'stances' are then often more difficult to describe, but the process is more challenging and entertaining.

BOX 35

Stances

12.6 Imperative symbols

Positive or negative commands: free composition of sentences, based on symbol cues; oral or written.

Materials: Individual copies of sheets of international symbols, as in *Box 36.*

Procedure: Using fairly well-known or obvious symbols (*Box 36a*), ask students to tell you what each one is telling you to do, or not to do:

> Stop!
> Come this way for ...
> Look out for ...

Or you may ask them to write down what they know; later teach each other, or you teach them, the right answers for the ones they did not know (given at the bottom of *Box 36a*).

Variations: Using the less immediately comprehensible symbols in *Box 36b*, ask the students in pairs or groups to invent interpretations, in the form of positive and negative commands. Who can invent the most entertaining/original/appropriate meaning for each?

The original meanings are listed at the bottom of *Box 36b*.

≫→

BOX 36a

Symbols (likely to be obvious or familiar)

Key to meanings (not exemplifying any specific grammatical form)
1 Stop, no entry   2 Don't drink the water   3 Dogs allowed   4 No smoking   5 Pass either side   6 Danger   7 Camping site
8 View or camera point   9 Cold spring   10 Maximum speed
11 Parking/waiting   12 Telephone   13 Stairs, up or down
14 Pedestrian crossing   15 No dogs   16 Compulsory stop
17 Put out campfires   18 Poison   19 Direction to be followed
20 Smoking permitted

BOX 36b

Symbols (likely to be unknown)

© Cambridge University Press 1988

Key to meanings (not exemplifying any specific grammatical form)
1 Press, interview room   2 Keep frozen   3 Open door or lid
4 Dry; heat   5 Blood donors   6 Telegrams   7 Registration
8 Lock   9 Lost child   10 Turning basin – manoeuvring (boats)
11 Protection and safety equipment   12 Agitate   13 Rendezvous point
14 Tourist activities   15 Pediatric clinic   16 Watersports area
17 Slow   18 Amphitheatre   19 Spin drying   20 Nature trail

12.7 Proverbs

Use of imperatives to give advice; reading and discussion.

Materials: Individual copies of a list of well-known proverbs using the imperative. A selection can be found in *Box 37*; or look up more in a book of proverbs (see BIBLIOGRAPHY, under *Other sources*).

Procedure: Go through the list explaining difficult vocabulary and making sure the meanings of the proverbs are clear. Ask each student to choose five favourite ones, and learn them by heart. Later, discuss: what are these proverbs in fact telling you to do? Is it always good advice? Can they think of parallel exhortations in their own language, translate them into English, and compare?

BOX 37

Proverbs in the imperative

1 Don't cry over spilt milk.
2 Don't put off to tomorrow what you can do today.
3 Make hay while the sun shines.
4 Do as you would be done by.
5 Don't count your chickens before they're hatched.
6 Don't cross your bridges before you come to them.
7 Save for a rainy day.
8 Never say die.
9 Don't put all your eggs in one basket.
10 When in Rome, do as the Romans do.
11 If at first you don't succeed, try try again.
12 Take care of the pennies and the pounds will take care of themselves.
13 Leave well alone.
14 Live and let live.
15 Don't look a gift horse in the mouth.
16 Don't wash your dirty linen in public.
17 Look before you leap.
18 Don't make a mountain out of a molehill.
19 Cut your coat according to your cloth.
20 If the cap fits, wear it.

© Cambridge University Press 1988

See also:
2.1 *Miming adverbs*;
17.5 *Games and their rules.*

13   Indirect speech

13.1   Reading reports

Reported (past) speech: reading and discussion of texts.

Materials: A pile of English newspaper cuttings reporting interviews.
Procedure: Give the students the cuttings (at least one each), and tell
them to copy out, or mark in fluorescent pen, instances of indirect
speech. You may need to help individuals with comprehension of more
difficult texts. Each student then reads out a selection of his or her
sentences, the others try to guess the speaker and/or circumstances.

13.2   Reporting interviews

Reported (past) speech, mainly statements: production of generalized
written account of oral dialogue.

Procedure: Invite a volunteer student to the front of the class and
interview him or her for two or three minutes (about a hobby, for
example, or an interesting experience, or future plan). Then ask
students to write down, in indirect speech, all they can remember of
what the interviewee said, as if they were writing a report for a
newspaper. In groups, they then combine their data to produce brief
reports.
Variations: For homework, ask students to interview someone outside
the class on a specific topic agreed on in advance – for example, their
views on smoking, or fashion, or a topical event – and then write a
report on it. The interview itself may be conducted in the native
language if you are teaching in a non-English speaking environment, as
long as the reporting is done in English. The reports, after being
corrected, may be 'published' as a mini-survey.
Comment: By careful selection of topic you can get students to concentrate on practising a specific tense. For example, an interview about
future plans will produce sentences like:
   She said she *would visit* New York.
One about past experiences will produce:
   He said he *had been* in great danger.

13.3 Quotation quiz

Reported (past) speech, mainly statements: transformation from direct (written) to indirect (written or spoken) speech.

Procedure: Give students a brief indirect-quotation quiz of your own:
    Who told Pharaoh to let his people go?
    Who asked who had been eating his porridge?
After identifying the source, reconstruct the original quotation. Then ask each student to prepare two or three (direct) quotations they think will be familiar to other members of the class. These do not have to be originally in English, they may be translations; they may be generally well-known sayings, or 'in'-jokes familiar locally, or something said recently by someone the students know. This can be done for homework the night before; if done in class, then have a reserve list of your own ready (some ideas in *Box 38*) to help students who cannot readily think of any.

Students then get together in groups of four or five to prepare indirect-quotation quizzes, each question of which has to begin 'Who said that...?' (or any reasonable alternative, such as 'Who asked if...' or 'Who requested/ordered ... to ...?'). When all the groups have at least seven or eight questions ready, quizzes are exchanged, and groups try to answer each other's questions. At the end, all groups read aloud their original questions and check answers.

⟫→

BOX 38

Quotations

1 'Let my people go!' (Moses)
2 'I can resist everything except temptation.' (Oscar Wilde)
3 'England is a nation of shopkeepers.' (Napoleon)
4 'I have nothing to offer but blood, toil, tears and sweat.' (Winston Churchill)
5 'I came, I saw, I conquered.' (Julius Caesar)
6 'We are not amused.' (Queen Victoria)
7 'You can fool all the people some of the time, and some of the people all of the time, but you cannot fool all of the people all of the time.' (Abraham Lincoln)
8 'I cannot tell a lie, I did it with my little hatchet.' (George Washington)
9 'The report of my death was an exaggeration.' (Mark Twain)
10 'Workers of the world, unite!' (Karl Marx)
11 'Let them eat cake!' (Marie Antoinette)
12 'I think, therefore I am.' (Descartes)
13 'An oral contract isn't worth the paper it's written on.' (Sam Goldwyn)
14 'That's one small step for a man, one giant leap for mankind.' (Neil A. Armstrong)
15 'All animals are equal, but some animals are more equal than others.' (George Orwell)

13.4 Correspondence

Indirect questions, statements, requests: transformation of short texts from direct to indirect speech; written.

Procedure: Give each student the name of one other student, and tell them to write a brief message to him or her, and sign it. It may be a question:

Are you enjoying this course?

or a statement:

You are looking very nice today!

or a request:

Can you lend me five pounds?

The notes are delivered, brief answers written (on the same piece of paper) and sent back, and so on until several lines of correspondence have been put together. All this should be done in silence (if possible!). Each student then takes the correspondence he or she initiated, and prepares it for reporting – that is to say, writes out an indirect speech version:

> I asked Anna if she was enjoying this course. She told me it was all right...

Then you take in the completed reports for checking. In the next lesson, pick out some of the more entertaining, and invite the authors to read them aloud – or do so yourself (with their permission!).

13.5 People used to believe

Indirect past statements contrasted with present; oral or written brainstorm, based on cues.

Procedure: Introduce the topic of the advance of scientific knowledge, and give some examples of what people used to believe:

> People used to believe that the world was flat.
> People used to believe that you could turn iron into gold.

and contrast them with:

> But now we know that the world is round.
> But now we know that gold is an element.

Ask students to think of some more examples of contrasts between past belief and present knowledge, and write up on the board only the second half of each ('But now we know that...'). When you have a list of ten or more such items on the board, ask students to recall, orally or in writing, what the first half was ('People used to believe...').

Variations: Suggest that students recall their own youthful misconceptions ('I used to believe that...'), and share them with one another.

13.6 What would you need to know?

Indirect questions, also the construction *know how to...* (or *...whol when/where/whether to...*); oral or written brainstorm, based on cues; optional discussion follow-up.

Procedure: Ask the class what they think a new student needs to know on entering the present course/school; suggest they use the question words *who/where*, etc.

> You need to know where the secretary's office is.
> You need to know when to come to class.

Write up their ideas on the board. Then ask each student to think of a field of activity he or she knows something about – his or her profession, a hobby, an aspect of his or her way of life – and make a quick list of things someone new to it would need to know. If you were taking up sailing, for example:

You would need to know how to swim.

You would need to know a good place to sail.

Then students may describe to you and the rest of the class the necessary knowledge for 'their' fields, or tell each other in pairs or small groups.

Variations: If working in pairs or groups, the listeners may, of course, contribute or criticize:

Wouldn't I need to know ... ?

Why would I need to know that?

and a discussion may develop.

13.7 Tell me what they said

Indirect questions, statements, requests in present or past; written transformations from direct to indirect speech.

Materials: Pictures of people talking to each other (*Box 39*), displayed to all the class, or distributed to individual students. You can also use pictures from your coursebook, or ones cut from magazines.

Procedure: Take one of the pictures, and discuss what the people have been saying to one another (formulated in indirect speech):

He's asking her to marry him and she's telling him she won't.

Then ask each student to select any picture and write down what he or she thinks the characters are saying, or said (you can, of course, decide arbitrarily whether the pictures represent past or present action, depending on what tenses you want to practise). They then read out their reported dialogues, and the rest of the class try to identify which picture is being described.

Variations: Further such exercises can be done for homework, in which case you can read out some of the reported dialogues the next day for the class to guess the picture.

BOX 39

Dialogue pictures

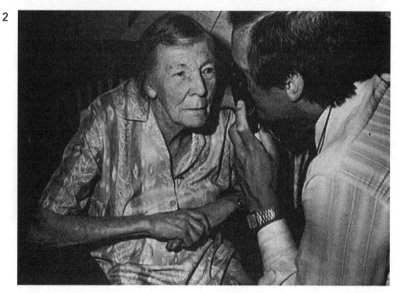

>>>→

BOX 39 continued

3

4

See also:
33.1 *What to do.*

14 -ING form of the verb

14.1 My tastes

Love/hate/don't mind + VERB + *-ing*; brief written responses based on set pattern.

Procedure: Give each student a loose piece of paper and ask them to write down one thing they love doing, one thing they hate doing and one thing they don't mind doing. Do the same yourself. Take in the papers, then read them out one by one, and see if the class can identify each student – and you – by likes and dislikes.

14.2 Opinion questionnaire

Verbs that take following VERB + *-ing* (for example, 'I enjoy dancing', or 'he risked falling') used in set questions and answers; reading and oral interaction.

Materials: Multiple copies of brief questionnaires, such as those shown in *Box 40*. It is best to make up your own version, based on controversial topics appropriate to your own teaching context; my examples are suitable for young adult classes.

Procedure: The class is divided into groups, each of which gets a different questionnaire; each member of a group has a copy of it. The groups then disperse and re-form in such a way that there is at least one representative of each of the original groups in every new group. Participants take turns to ask all other member of the new groups their questions, and jot down the answers. They then re-form into the original groupings to pool the answers they have collected, and formulate their results into complete sentences, such as:

    20% of our population enjoy smoking.

    30% of our population like driving fast.

and report back to the class. These results may later be written up neatly and displayed.

BOX 40

Questionnaire 1

	Yes	No
1 Do you enjoy smoking?		
2 Do you mind other people smoking near you?		
3 Do you approve of smoking as a habit?		
4 (For smokers) Could you stop smoking easily?		
5 Should we forbid smoking in public places?		

Questionnaire 2

	Yes	No
1 Do you enjoy listening to pop music?		
2 (If so), at what age did you start enjoying it?		
3 Do you mind other people listening to loud pop music near you?		
4 Do you like singing pop songs yourself?		
5 Do you prefer listening to pop music to watching television?		

BOX 40   continued

Questionnaire 3

	Yes	No
1 Do you enjoy listening to classical music?		
2 (If so), at what age did you start enjoying it?		
3 Do you mind other people listening to loud classical music near you?		
4 Do you like or play (classical music) yourself?		
5 Do you prefer listening to classical music to watching television?		

Questionnaire 4

	Yes	No
1 Do you enjoy drinking wine with a meal?		
2 Do you enjoy drinking spirits (like brandy) between meals?		
3 Could you easily do without drinking (alcoholic drinks) at all?		
4 Do you always avoid getting drunk?		
5 Do you mind people getting drunk in your company?		

BOX 40   continued

Questionnaire 5

	Yes	No
1 Do you enjoy driving?		
2 Do you like driving fast?		
3 Do you dislike other people overtaking you?		
4 Do you ever risk being fined for speeding?		
5 Do you disapprove of people racing each other on the highway?		

© Cambridge University Press 1988

14.3   How could you do it?

The -*ing* form of the verb after prepositions; brainstorm, based on set pattern; mostly oral; optional discussion follow-up.

Procedure: Suggest a simple task:

How do you get someone to come to you?

and ask for a straightforward solution using *by* + VERB + -*ing*:

By calling them.

Then make it more complicated by adding a condition, also represented by a preposition + VERB + -*ing*:

How do you get someone to come to you without speaking?

The students may have several solutions:

By getting someone else to call them.

By writing them a note.

By making a sign with your hand.

Give new vocabulary as needed.

Some examples of simple tasks with various possible complications are given in *Box 41.*

Variations: Give students, in groups, several such 'complicated' problems, and tell them these are initiative, or ingenuity, tests: which group can find the most effective (or economical, or original) solutions? Results to be judged by you, or discussed by the class as a whole.

Later, students may be asked to design their own problems, to be exchanged and solved, and/or discussed.

BOX 41

How could you ...

1 ... get someone to come to you (without speaking, or while facing the other way)?
2 ... open a door (without touching the handle, or before reaching it)?
3 ... pick up a pencil (without touching it, or while keeping your eyes shut)?
4 ... sit on a chair (without bending your knees, or without looking at it)?
5 ... open a tin (without using a tin-opener, or while holding one hand behind your back)?
6 ... get into your home (after losing the key, or without opening a door or window)?

---

15 Interrogatives

15.1 Dialogues

Simple interrogative, affirmative and negative forms, within dialogues; oral repetition of forms learnt by heart.

Materials: Short conversations between two speakers consisting of four to six utterances, representing some kind of communicative event. For example:
> A: What are you doing?
> B: I'm going outside.
> A: Why? (pause) Why are you going outside?
> B: None of your business.

Your coursebook will probably supply further examples; or see BIBLIOGRAPHY.

Procedure: The dialogue is presented orally – with or without written reinforcement – and learnt by heart by the students, preferably during the lesson through various kinds of repetition (choral, pair, individual), reiterating or answering utterances said by the teacher. It is then performed either by a single pair of students in front of the class, or by all the students, in pairs, simultaneously. The dialogue should be reviewed in later lessons in order to consolidate learning.

Variations: Just repeating dialogues as they stand can be boring. It is a good idea to vary them by introducing different stage directions. These can apply only to speed, tone or volume ('Do the dialogue fast/slowly ... in a high/low voice ... loudly/softly ...') or they can apply to mood or personality ('Do the dialogue angrily ... sadly ... laughingly ... dramatically ... fearfully...'). You can even prescribe an entire situational context ('The dialogue is an exchange of code formulae by secret agents in hostile territory ... or a conversation between a teacher and student in a lesson ... or part of a marital quarrel...'). Such directions may be issued to the performers privately, and the rest of the class asked to guess what the situation is. In such ways the dialogue can be repeated many more times, familiarizing the learners more effectively with its forms, while maintaining interest.

Later, of course, the actual content can be varied: you can ask students to suggest alternatives to certain key words (for example, 'going outside' in the dialogue given as an example here can be replaced with 'reading a book', 'walking around', etc.), or further exchanges can be added to develop the situation in different ways.

A technique called *wrangling* can be used with two-utterance exchanges that express or imply some kind of conflict. For example:

A: Will you marry me?
B: Why should I?

Students work in pairs, each taking one of the 'parts' and argue with each other using **only** the exact words of their line. They try to wear each other down by repeating their utterances in turn, using as many varied kinds of emphasis as they can. The first to give up is the loser.

15.2 Choosing or composing comprehension questions

All kinds of questions on a reading passage; reading and understanding; optionally, composing new questions.

Procedure: Using a conventional reading passage-plus-comprehension-questions text (preferably one from your coursebook that you are going to do anyway) invite students to select those questions they think are most sensible for testing comprehension, and to cross out the rest – leaving about half the original number. They may do this individually, in pairs or in groups. They go on to answer the questions they have chosen.

Variations: After reading a passage, invite the class to suggest their own comprehension questions. Write up all suggestions on the board, and then ask students to whittle down the number of questions as described above.

15.3 Find someone with the answer

'WH' questions; reading and identifying spoken answers.

Materials: Slips of paper with simple 'WH' questions on them; separate slips with corresponding answers. There should be one copy of each question and one of each answer; in total, rather more pairs of slips than there are students in the class. For example, for a class of 20 students, you should have about 30 questions and 30 corresponding answers (as in *Boxes 42a* and *b*).

Procedure: Each student gets one question slip and one answer slip. In 'fluid pairs', students ask each other 'their' questions, giving 'their' answers in response – though these will usually be inappropriate. When a question does get a correct answer, the two students put their slips together and come to you. You check that they are right, and take in the slips. A pair of students left without any slips at all gets fresh ones from your reserve pile, until there are none left. The activity goes on until all question and answer slips have been paired off.

BOX 42a

Questions and answers

Questions

What language do they speak in Brazil?	What colour is the sky?
What language do they speak in Australia?	Where is Montreal?
What language do they speak in Quebec?	Where is Geneva?
What was the name of the first man?	Where is Teheran?
Who was King Solomon's father?	What colours is a panda?
Who led the Israelites out of Egypt?	What colour is a lemon?
What is the first month of the year?	What is three times six?

BOX 42a continued

How many tens are there in a hundred?	Who wrote *Tom Sawyer*?
How many grams are there in a kilo?	Who wrote *Winnie the Pooh*?
How many legs does a fly have?	Who wrote *Macbeth*?
How many legs does a spider have?	What is seven plus eight?
How many legs does a horse have?	Where did Cleopatra live?
How many days are there in a week?	How many days are there in June?
What is cheese made from?	What is bread made from?
How many litres are there in a kilo of water?	Who discovered America?

BOX 42b

Answers

Portuguese	English	French
Adam	King David	Moses
January	Ten	A thousand
Six	Eight	Four
Seven	Milk	One
Blue	In Canada	In Switzerland
In Iran	Black and white	Yellow
Eighteen	Mark Twain	A. A. Milne
Shakespeare	Fifteen	In Egypt
Thirty	Flour	Columbus

© Cambridge University Press 1988

15.4 Questionnaires

Mostly 'yes/no' questions; reading and answering set questions, mostly orally. Optional follow-up: composing new questions.

Materials: Individual copies of questionnaires on a topic that interests the class, based on vocabulary they know or can guess. Often the most effective are the 'know yourself' type, with questions designed to elicit information about the answerer's personality. These may be in the form of one question with various endings, or a series of different questions (both types shown in *Box 43*). Examples of different kinds of

BOX 43a

Questionnaire about yourself

What are you like?

Answer code: 1=Yes, very (much/many); 2=Yes, quite;
3=So-so; 4=Not very (much/many); 5=Not at all

1 Are you . . .	1 2 3 4 5
. . . sure of yourself?	1 2 3 4 5
. . . interested in other people?	1 2 3 4 5
. . . usually happy?	1 2 3 4 5
. . . a hard worker?	1 2 3 4 5
. . . intelligent?	1 2 3 4 5
2 Do you often help other people?	1 2 3 4 5
3 Do you care if people like you or not?	1 2 3 4 5
4 Have you got a lot of friends?	1 2 3 4 5
5 Can you be patient with stupid people?	1 2 3 4 5

© Cambridge University Press 1988

questionnaires in *Boxes 4* and *40*, pages *50* and *144*; see also BIBLIOGRAPHY.

Procedure: Each student gets a sheet of the questions, and writes his or her answers; or students can work in pairs, asking each other the questions and noting down answers; or in 'fluid pairs', asking different partners each time.

Variations: In groups, each student writes down his or her own answers, and then further sets of answers for each other member of the group (*Box 43b*), according to his or her own estimation of the other member's personality. Participants then compare what they think of themselves with what their co-students think of them: very revealing! But only to be attempted if relationships within the class are fairly warm and comfortable.

Instead of the questionnaire being supplied ready-made, it may be designed by the students, working in pairs or groups, on the basis of a set objective (some ideas in *Box 43c*). The question forms used should be checked by you before the questionnaires are administered and filled in.

BOX 43b

Questionnaire about yourself

What makes you do things?

Answer code: 1=Yes, definitely;   2=Yes, probably;
3=Sometimes;   4=Not usually;   5=No, never

	Myself	(Names of others in group)			
1 Do you try harder to do something because ...					
... people will like you if you do?					
... you will get money for it?					

BOX 43b continued

	Myself	(Names of others in group)			
... you enjoy doing it?					
... you believe it is a good thing to do?					
... you are afraid of what will happen if you don't?					
2 Is it important to you to know people think your work is good?					
3 Is a job easier for you if you are working with other people?					
4 Would you like to be famous?					
5 Can you make yourself work hard at things you don't really like doing?					

BOX 43c

You could design questionnaires about ...

... How healthy are you?
... How good a student are you?
... How good a friend are you?
... How creative are you?
... Was your childhood a happy one?
... What are your political opinions? (left/right/centre)
... How do you feel about yourself? (self-esteem)
... How good is your family life?
... Are you content with your life?
... How well do you get on with other people?
... Are you optimistic/pessimistic?

15.5   Common denominator

'Yes/no' questions; oral responses, based on set patterns.

Procedure: Think of a certain feature that may be common to various objects, ('roundness', for example), and put one such object into a sentence:

I love ... the sun.

Students then try to find out what your 'common denominator' is by asking questions based on the original sentence. A student who thinks you are thinking of 'hot' might ask:

Do you love ... fire?

and one who thinks it is 'something in the sky' might ask:

Do you love ... clouds?

to both of which you answer 'no'. A question such as:

Do you love ... an orange?

however, since you are thinking of 'round', obviously gets the answer 'yes'.

The guessers only have one 'direct question' – for example:

Is the answer 'round'?

– so they have to be very sure that they are right before asking it – which means asking several verifying 'Do you love ... ?' questions even after they are fairly sure they know the answer.

Variations: The original sentence does not, of course, have to begin 'I love ...' You can vary it according to the kind of verb, or tense, you want to practise in the interrogative. Some possible variations are in *Box 44*, together with some more ideas for common denominators.

156

BOX 44

Possible base sentences

1 I / my friend love(s) ...
2 We're going on a picnic tomorrow, and we'll take ...
3 I'm reading a book about ...
4 Yesterday Jeremy went for a walk, and he saw ...
5 I'm going shopping soon, and I'm going to buy ...
6 In our kitchen there is ...
7 I would like to have ...

Possible common denominators

round	square	soft	hard	long	short

smaller or larger than a person	red/yellow/green/blue

made of metal/wood etc.	is in this classroom

floats on water	can fly	can be eaten or drunk

can be held in the hand	is a machine

breaks if it is dropped	makes a noise

is made of animal (or vegetable, or mineral) substance

begins or ends with a certain letter	is a machine

contains a certain letter	contains five or more letters

begins with the same letter as the name of the guesser

the same word exists in the student's native language

Activities

15.6 Guessing

'Yes/no' questions; oral brainstorming.

Procedure: The teacher or a volunteer student chooses or is given an item to be guessed: this may be an object, person, activity, place or event. The rest of the class asks 'yes/no' questions, to be answered by the 'knower', until the item is guessed.

> A: Is it in the classroom?
> B: No.
> C: Can we eat it?
> B: Yes.
> D: Is it round?
> B: Yes.
> E: Is it an apple?
> B: Yes.

Sometimes the knower may begin by giving a set hint: whether the item is a person, animal or thing; whether it is male, female, neuter, singular or plural; whether it is animal, vegetable or mineral.

Variations: The activity can be made more brisk and motivating by the introduction of a limit on the number of questions that may be asked ('You have to guess the answer in not more than 20 questions'), or on the time available ('You have two minutes to guess the answer').

One well-known variation on the guessing game is *Coffeepot*. The knower chooses or is given a verb; the rest of the class try to guess it by asking questions in which the word *coffeepot* is substituted for the verb, with appropriate suffixes added if necessary:

> Does an animal coffepot?
> Do I like coffeepotting?

As a written follow-up, students compose a series of questions, together with the appropriate answers ('yes' or 'no', plus, possibly, short 'tag' answers), intended to lead to a certain solution. You, then, have not only to check the grammar of the questions but also guess the solutions. For example, a student might write:

> Does it have four legs? No.
> Does it fly? No.
> Does it swim? Yes.
> Can we eat it? Yes.

Similar sets of questions composed by students may be brought to class for students to exchange between themselves, and guess each other's items; or both writing and reading may be done as a classroom activity.

Comment: Note that in the full-class spoken version of this activity, the knower, who gives only brief answers, should be a single person (or possibly two), while the bulk of the class should be asking the questions. If it is done the other way round, the load on the guesser is too heavy while most of the class have too little to do – with the result that the process slows down and becomes tedious, and the practice is inefficient.

For younger classes it is a good idea to have the item to be guessed physically represented in some way, not just imagined: written on a piece of paper, depicted, or itself actually present in the room. If pictures are used, then the lucky guesser can be given the picture (temporarily) as a symbolic prize.

15.7   Quizzes

'WH' questions; reading and answering given questions; optional follow-up: composing new questions.

Materials: Individual copies of a general knowledge quiz (example in *Box 45*). The game 'Trivial Pursuit' is a good source of further questions.

Procedure: Tell the class there is a lot of criticism of the lack of general cultural knowledge of the present generation of students. How much does this class know? Tell them to try to fill in the answers to the quiz, individually and then, possibly, helping each other in pairs or groups. (You may need to run through the questions first to make sure they are understood.) Then they read out questions, and check answers. How did the class, as a whole, do?

Variations: Without looking at the original quiz, how many of the questions (and their correct answers) can they recall later in the lesson – or the following day?

Ask them to suggest – in class or for homework – another three/four/ten questions they think could have been included in a quiz of this kind.

Suggest they compose a similar quiz for you, the teacher, on a local topic on which they are experts and you, possibly, are not.

»»→

BOX 45

Cultural knowledge quiz

1 Where is Toronto?
2 Who spoke Latin?
3 How do you find out the area of a circle?
4 Who said 'I think, therefore I am'?
5 How many players are there in a football team?
6 Where can you find the words 'In the beginning ...'?
7 Who was Elvis Presley?
8 What was Sherlock Holmes' profession?
9 When did the Second World War start?
10 What country was Hamlet prince of?
11 How do elephants sleep – standing up or lying down?
12 What are the five senses?
13 What kind of an animal is a dingo?
14 What is a gondola?
15 What is the capital of Ethiopia?
16 In which city is the White House?
17 What is the name of Mickey Mouse's girlfriend?
18 How often are the Olympic Games held?
19 Where did Peter Pan take Wendy?
20 What happened to Pompeii?

© Cambridge University Press 1988

Brief answers

1 In Canada   2 The Romans   3 πr^2 4 Descartes
5 Eleven   6 Genesis, ch. 1, v.1   7 A pop singer
8 Detective   9 1939   10 Denmark   11 Standing up
12 Sight, hearing, touch, smell, taste   13 A wild dog
14 A boat (in Venice)   15 Addis Ababa   16 Washington
17 Minnie Mouse   18 Every four years   19 To the
Never-never land   20 It was destroyed by a volcano

15.8 Filling in forms

All kinds of interrogatives in the present: constructing oral questions on basis of brief written cues; reading and oral interaction.

Materials: Individual copies of simple forms, as in *Box 46.*

Procedure: Tell students (to imagine) that the school's records have been lost or destroyed, and you need personal details about each one of them for the new files. They should sit in pairs and note down details of each other's identity and background, as demanded by the form. All such information must be given only in response to a proper question: thus, given the cue 'Age', the asker must say:

How old are you?

During the process of supplying the information, the answerers may help or correct the askers in their questioning. Before giving in the filled-in forms, each student should check that his or her partner has in fact filled in the information correctly.

Variations: Each answerer has to give two **false** pieces of information in response to the question asked; at the end, each student tries to identify his or her partner's lies. (This variation is, obviously, only feasible if the students know each other fairly well – and is one way of getting to know each other even better!)

Later, students may role-play a different person: a celebrity, a fictional character, or a locally-known personality – and answer the questions in their 'new' persona. Later, read out data from one or more of the filled-in forms, and see if the class as a whole can identify which student was the real answerer.

≫→

BOX 46

Form to fill in

Surname:	First name(s):

Age:	Married: Yes/no	Profession:

Place of birth:

Home address:

Telephone No.

Address at work:

Telephone No.

Names of children (if any):

Interests:

© Cambridge University Press 1988

15.9 Don't say yes or no

'Yes/no' questions; free oral interaction.

Procedure: A volunteer stands in front of the class, and the rest of the students fire questions at him or her designed to elicit the answer 'Yes' or 'No'. The answerer tries to avoid saying these words, substituting acceptable paraphrases. If, however, 'Yes' or 'No' is said, the answerer is 'out', and another volunteer takes his or her place.

15.10 Preparing interviews

All kinds of interrogatives; free composition of questions for an interview; optional writing of questions, followed by oral interaction.

Procedure: Tell students they are to interview you for a television 'chat' programme, and must prepare a set of ten to 20 questions to elicit information they want. Give them ten or 15 minutes to do so, helping them with new vocabulary where necessary. You may wish them to write out the questions in full, or just jot them down in brief note form. They then interview you.

Variations: Later, give each student the name of another student to interview, and ask them to prepare their questions and then get into pairs to perform the interviews. They may later describe to the class some of the questions they asked and their answers, or write them up for homework. If, however, the students know each other very well, then just getting general information about each other may be rather pointless. So ask each student to suggest something he or she is particularly interested in, or well-informed about, and would be willing to be interviewed about; then students get into pairs to interview each other about their respective fields of interest – and, again, report back to the class. As far as possible, try to let students choose their own partners, finding topics of mutual interest.

Alternatively, give students fictional characters or celebrities to prepare interview questions for, and then ask for volunteers to role-play the interviewees. Each student may choose a different person to interview from a list provided by you (some suggestions in *Box 47*); or all may prepare questions for one person. In the latter case, one student, or you yourself, role-play(s) the interviewee, and all the others take turns asking the questions.

BOX 47

People you could interview (in role-play)

Well-known personalities in politics, the current news, entertainment, sports, the arts, broadcasting.

Local people: students or teachers from the school, well-known personalities from the community.

People who have something unusual about them: a mother of 20 children; a professional stuntman/woman; the inventor of a cure for cancer; a beauty queen/king; the possessor of a pet elephant; a woman with three husbands / man with three wives; a person 2.1 metres tall; a person who can breathe underwater; a (male) children's nanny; a (female) bus-driver.

15.11   What are they saying?

All kinds of interrogatives; free composition of questions and answers, based on picture cue; orally and/or in writing.

Materials: Pictures of people talking to one another, as in *Box 39*, page 141. Each student may have a copy, or they may be displayed, if big enough, at the front of the class. You can also use cut-out magazine pictures, or cartoons with 'balloons' to show speech – in which case you blank out the original dialogue.

Procedure: Tell the students that one of the characters is asking a question and the other is answering, and ask them to imagine what is being said. You may give some suggested 'answers' in advance and ask students to imagine the questions; or ask students to invent both questions and answers. Suggestions may be written or given orally. Sometimes you may be able to put together students' suggestions to form longer dialogues.

See also:
1.1   *Finding twins*;
18.2   *Combining arrangement*;
18.3   *Picture differences*;
22.1   *What were you doing last night? (1)*;
23.8   *What really happened?*;
23.10   *Alibi*;
31.3   *Written enquiries*.

16 Is/are, there is/there are

16.1 Describing pictures (1)

Use of *is/are* or *there is/there are* to describe a scene; oral brainstorm, optional written follow-up.

Materials: Large pictures that can easily be seen by all the class, preferably in colour and with plenty of clearly delineated detail; or individual smaller copies of the same. There are some good published pictures of various sizes suitable for this activity (see BIBLIOGRAPHY); cut-out magazine pictures are cheaper, but often not large and clear enough for full-class interaction. Or you may find suitable material in your own coursebook, either within the book itself or as supplementary flash cards or posters. Some examples for enlarging or copying (not in colour, unfortunately!) may be found in *Box 48*. Whatever you choose, make sure that most of the items depicted are within the vocabulary range of the class.

Procedure: Invite the students to say as much as they can about the picture, using *(There) is* or *(There) are*. Have a defined objective: 20 sentences in all, or as many as the class can manage in three minutes. Alternatively, show the picture for two minutes, then hide it and ask students to recall its content.

Variations: The same can, of course, be done in writing; or the writing can be done as a follow-up. It is sometimes a good idea to give the students two or three minutes before the spoken brainstorm to jot down some ideas: then when the speaking does start, there are plenty of contributions ready.

One variation is to display two pictures of roughly similar subjects – but by no means identical (*Box 10*, page 67) – and to ask students to suggest similarities, or differences, or both; in this case each contribution has two clauses:

> The horse in Picture B is white, but the horse in Picture A is black.

It is possible, of course, to ask questions instead of making statements about the picture. It is better if such questions are **not** simply alternative forms of statements, whose answer is obvious from the picture, but genuine uncertainties, which can then be answered imaginatively by other students.

BOX 48

Pictures for describing

1

2

BOX 48 continued

3

16.2 Describing pictures (2)

Use of *is/are* or *there is/there are* to describe a scene; oral brainstorm.

Materials: Two or three different pictures, of a similar type to that suggested for the previous activity, but small enough to be used for group work. You may need two or more copies of each if you have more than about 15 students in your class.

Procedure: After they have had a little practice in the full-class picture brainstorm, as described in *Describing pictures (1)* above, divide the students into groups. Give each group a picture and ask them to produce as many (*is/are*) sentences about that picture as possible within a given time limit – say, three minutes. One member of the group has to record the number of sentences – either jotting down a tick for each sentence, or actually writing it out. I prefer ticks, since the full writing out slows things down, lessens the volume of practice for most of the group, and frustrates those who are waiting to contribute. The groups then report how many sentences they produced.

After one such round, pictures are exchanged, and the process is repeated, each group trying to better its previous result (number of sentences produced). Then, possibly, the same process yet again (three rounds are usually enough!).

16.3 Picture dictation

Use of *is/are* or *there is/there are* to describe a scene; oral brainstorm.

Procedure: Draw a large rectangular frame on the board (or overhead projector), and invite students to tell you what to draw in it. You might start by suggesting it is a room, then saying 'there's a table in the room' and drawing it in. Students suggest further details:

There's a vase on the table.

The vase is blue.

Variations: You may, of course, invite students to do the drawing, but this tends to slow things down somewhat; better to do the sketching yourself, even if it is very unartistic, and gain more time for language practice. An alternative is to use prepared cut-out drawings: cardboard ones for a felt- or clip-board, or bits of acetate film for laying on the overhead projector – this, of course, both guides and limits the kinds of contributions available to the students.

The exercise can be made more interesting by asking students to describe not just a conventional scene, but an unusual one: an extremely untidy room, for example, or their ideal classroom, or an outdoor scene on an imaginary alien planet.

16.4 Find a twin picture

Use of *is/are* or *there is/there are* to identify features of a scene; constructing interrogative, negative or affirmative sentences; oral interaction.

Materials: A set of simple black-and-white pictures showing various combinations of between six and ten components: say, a table, a bird, a tree, an apple, a dog, a cat, an egg. These are fairly easily made by copying sketches of the components on separate pieces of acetate film, laying them in a basic arrangement on the photocopier and copying, then changing the position or direction of one component for each subsequent copy. You may make further variations, after the pictures have been copied, by colouring in or slightly altering some of the components by hand. Make **two** copies of each variation. In all, there should be enough to give every student one picture and still have ten or so in reserve. Examples in *Box 49*.

Procedure: Give each student one picture, which they are not allowed to show each other. Each student then has to find someone who has the exact duplicate of his or her picture: they do this by describing their pictures to each other, or asking questions:

There's a bird in the tree.
Is your cat black?
Where is your dog?

BOX 49

Pictures with differences

>>>→

Activities

Students who have found duplicates bring them to you; you check they are right, and give them further pictures from the reserve, until all are gone. The activity ends when all the pictures are paired.

Variations: The activity can be made slightly longer if there are **three** copies of each picture. Each student then has to find two others with the same picture.

BOX 49   continued

© Cambridge University Press 1988

16.5   Reverse guessing

Use of *is/are* with third person pronouns to describe people or simple objects; oral or written brainstorm.

Procedure: Choose the name of a person known to all the class, or a simple object (or group of objects), and tell all but one of the students what it is. The student who does not know then has to guess it, but does **not** ask any questions. It is up to the rest of the class to supply enough hints to enable him or her to guess correctly.

It is in the classroom.

She is tall and thin.

They are made of wood.

Comment: You may wish at first to limit sentences specifically to those exemplifying the use of *is/are*; but at a later stage, let the participants use whatever constructions they like. This will produce more interesting and varied sentences, and the use of *is/are* when it does occur – and it does! – will be more natural.

See also:

3.1 *Expanding headlines*;

8.3 *Kim's game.*

17 Modals

17.1 Guessing by abilities

Use of *can/can't* to describe abilities; oral brainstorm, with optional written follow-up.

Procedure: Choose the name of an object, an animal, or a person well known to the class. Tell all the class but one what it is. The student who does not know has to guess, with the help of hints suggested by the others, based on what the subject *can* or *can't do,* or what we *can* or *can't* do with it. For example, if the subject is 'koala bear', students might say:

> It can climb trees.
> It can carry its baby.
> You can't buy one in a shop.

They might occasionally need a new word – supply it as needed. The guesser may also ask *can/can't* questions, but may not guess what the subject actually is until the other students have given all their hints.

Variations: For homework, students describe a subject of their own choosing in this way for you to guess – or for other students to guess in the following lesson.

17.2 Uses of an object

Use of *can, could* to describe possibilities; oral brainstorming.

Materials: A picture of a simple object, or (better) the object itself. Examples in *Box 24*, page 95.

Procedure: Invite the students to suggest as many original uses for the object as they can, using *can* or *could* (whichever you want to practise). For example, if the object is a pen, students might suggest:

> You can use it to dig holes.
> You could scratch your head with it.

After initial demonstration with the full class, divide the students into groups, and give each group an object. They have three or four minutes to think up all the uses they can, noted by a 'secretary'. Help them with new vocabulary as necessary. Later, the groups report back their suggestions, which are usually entertaining enough in themselves to provide interest; or the activity can be made into a competition between groups to see who can produce the most ideas.

Variations: In lower-level classes, limited usually to the modal *can* in this activity, you can widen the range of possible sentences by saying that anything at all you can do with the object is acceptable. For example:

You can hold it.

You can put it on the table.

With more advanced classes, however, I find it better to lay down that the sentences must express an actual, feasible (though not necessarily likely!) **use** of the object (as in the examples under *Procedure* above): this is more of a challenge, and produces more varied, interesting contributions.

17.3   Desert island equipment

Use of *can/could/may/might* to express possibilities; free composition of sentences, based on situation and object cue; oral.

Materials: A pile of small pictures of objects. You could use drawings such as those in *Box 5*, page 56, or bits of magazine pictures, or published small pictures for language learning (see BIBLIOGRAPHY).

Procedure: Tell the students they are stranded on a desert island. They have before them a pile of items, each of which they may keep if they can find a convincing use for it in the desert island situation. In turn, each student picks up a picture, and suggests how he or she *can/may/might/could* use whatever it depicts. For example, a student who picks up a picture of a shirt might suggest:

We could use the shirt as a flag to signal to ships.

After initial full-class demonstration, this is best done in groups (with some help from you with vocabulary). The students themselves decide which uses are 'legitimate' and which not.

Variations: The activity may be presented as an inter-student or inter-group competition. Or neither; the challenge of finding uses is often motivating enough in itself, and groups can be asked at the end to share their most original ideas, or tell the class what they *can* do, in general, on their island as a result of having all this equipment.

Comment: This is similar to 17.2 *Uses of an object*, but slightly more advanced: sentences are likely to be longer and more complex ('If we ... then we might/could...').

17.4 Modal symbols

Use of *can/can't/must/mustn't* to express permission, obligation and prohibition; oral and written responses to simple graphic cues.

Materials: Individual copies of a sheet of international symbols, like those in *Box 36a*, page 133; or the same shown on the overhead projector.

Procedure: Using the more well-known symbols (*Box 36a*), ask the students to tell you, or write down, what each symbol means, using *can, can't, must* or *mustn't*. Check the correct interpretation of each symbol.

Variations: Using the less obvious symbols (*Box 36b*), brainstorm possible interpretations for each one. Then you can either select with the class the one which is the most original, entertaining or convincing; or give them the correct interpretations at the end.

Ask the class to suggest warnings, suggestions, etc. that could be posted at different places in the school, and to devise symbols for them.

17.5 Games and their rules

Use of *may, may not, can, can't, must, mustn't* to define rules; free composition of sentences; oral or written.

Procedure: Choose a game that the students all know. Write up on the board some basic facts about it: the number of players, objective, equipment, amount of time and space needed. Give some basic vocabulary essential to a description of the game. Then invite students to list its rules, using modals such as *may, may not, can, can't, must, mustn't*. They may write down rules and later read them out, or go straight into oral suggestions.

Variations: Divide students into groups, and give each group a different (well-known) game; ask them to write down (as a group) as many rules as they can think of in ten minutes on a sheet of paper. They then exchange papers, and correct and add to each other's lists. And so on, until all groups have seen all papers. When you have checked the results these may be copied out and displayed.

If you have a class of students from various different background cultures, then each can write about games from home that they think other students may not be familiar with; then describe them to each other.

Imaginative students may be asked to make up their own games: original types of races, or competitions based on school or domestic activities.

17.6 Advice for a novice

Use of all kinds of modals to give advice; composing affirmative, negative and interrogative sentences; oral and written.

Procedure: Ask students to write down any advice they would give a student – or teacher – entering the course, or the school, for the first time: the kinds of things they *should* or *shouldn't* do, or *must* or *mustn't* do.

> You must come to work on time.
> You shouldn't make private phone calls on the office phone.

Help individuals with new vocabulary as needed. Then hear their suggestions, list them on the board, and decide with them which are the most important three – or five – pieces of advice.

Variations: Ask each student to tell you one field of interest, or hobby, or profession, which he or she knows quite a lot about and could give advice on; write it on the board, by the student's name. Then each student chooses two or three of these topics that they know little or nothing about, but are interested in, and prepare some questions to ask about them. Questions might begin with phrases like:

> Must I ... ?
> Can one ... ?
> Should I ... ?
> Might you ... ?

You may, of course, prescribe in advance which modals, or which phrases, you want the questions to be based on.

After about ten minutes of preparing questions, students then go to the 'experts' in the class to find out the answers; each one will be both asking (as 'novice') and answering (as 'expert').

Later, students describe, orally or in writing, interesting things they have learnt about the various topics.

17.7 Duties and privileges

Use of *can, may, can't, may not, must, mustn't, don't have to, should, shouldn't,* to define duties and privileges; free composition; general discussion as follow-up.

Procedure: Tell the class to imagine that they are responsible for finding a suitable candidate to fill a position they know something about: a new teacher or student, a school secretary, for example. They have to write out an informal job description which might serve as a letter for circulating among likely candidates, or as a basis for interview. The description should include all the duties and privileges associated with the position:

> You must be on duty at least seven hours a day.
>
> You can/may have a company car.

and qualities or qualifications that the candidate should have:

> You should have a friendly, warm personality.
>
> You must be able to drive.

They may do this individually or in small groups, pooling their ideas later. The resulting description may be written up and displayed, and/or furnish a basis for a general discussion.

Variations: For homework, students write about the duties and privileges of a job they are familiar with: what they do themselves as a profession, or one of their parents or other members of the family do.

17.8 Dilemmas

Use of all kinds of modals to express possibility, obligation, necessity; free discussion or writing.

Materials: A situation either described in language (spoken or written) or depicted in graphic form. For example: a moral dilemma of some kind, or a survival situation. Some examples are given in *Box 50*; or you could use pictures like those in *Box 28*, page 106; or letters from the advice column of an English-language magazine.

Procedure: Present the situation, and make sure it is clear to all students. Ask them to brainstorm comments, suggestions or questions in order to suggest possible, advisable or necessary courses of action. The verbs to be used may be dictated in advance: *must* or *have to*, *should* or *ought to*, *may*, *might* or *could*. Or the formulation of ideas may be left open to the students: the task will tend to generate modals anyway.

You may present the activity as a simple brainstorm, and accept any suggestion as a possibility, or try to find one 'best' solution.

Variations: Ask the students to role-play the situation in small groups: one of them is the person with the problem, the other members of the group are counsellors. Later, the groups describe the conclusions they reached, orally or in writing.

For homework, students may be asked to write a sentence or two on each of several situations, or explore the possibilities of one of them in detail. The title of the essay may dictate the kind of modal to be used, for example:

> What should I do?
>
> What may happen?

BOX 50

Dilemmas

1 Your car has a puncture, and you have just discovered that the spare tyre is flat. You are alone on a lonely road; night is falling.

2 You have noticed your best friend cheating in an end-of-term exam. A lot of kids cheat, but you and your friend have always been against it, up to now.

3 Your parents prefer your younger brother to you: they buy him more new things, and generally discriminate in his favour. If you protest, they get angry.

4 Your boyfriend/girlfriend said he or she could not come out with you this evening because of work; but you've just seen him or her coming out of a cinema hand in hand with another girl/boy.

5 You and your friends are mountain-climbing; you have been caught in a sudden thick fog, and are lost.

6 Your mother has had a stroke and is semi-paralyzed. She hates the idea of going into an institution, but needs constant care. You cannot afford a nurse, and do not want to give up your job.

7 Someone close to you, of your age, has got a fatal disease, and the doctors say there is no hope. She has asked you to help her end her life now.

8 You have been offered a well-paid job by a rich employer, and badly need the money; but people have told you that his business is dishonest.

9 You tried using an illegal drug, for the first time, at a party a year ago – hated it – and haven't touched the stuff since. But someone who saw you at the party threatens to tell the police if you don't pay them off.

10 A friend, while driving you in his car, hit someone crossing the road, and knocked them down. You told him to stop; he said the person wasn't badly hurt, and drove on.

11 You felt really ill last night, and rang your boss. He was very nice, and told you to take the day off. Today, you got up late, and now – at 10 a.m. – feel perfectly well.

12 You have put on a lot of weight, none of your clothes fit, and your doctor says you must diet. But you feel OK, and enjoy your food – also, you have to eat out a lot in your job.

17.9 Being polite

Use of modals to formulate polite requests and offers (*Would you (mind)...?, Could you...?, Shall I...?*, etc.); oral interaction.

Procedure: Discuss briefly the importance of the forms of courtesy, in an English-language culture and in the students' native culture(s). Then present a brief transaction in abrupt, direct commands/questions/comments, for example:

    A: Hey, you! Open this door!
    B: It's locked. Want me to get the key?
    A: Yeah. Get it. Fast.

and discuss how it could be made more polite, for example:

    A: Excuse me, would you open this door?
    B: I'm afraid it's locked. Shall I get the key?
    A: Please, if you wouldn't mind, as quickly as you can.

Then divide students into groups of four, give each a situation involving getting someone to do something (some examples in *Box 51*), and ask them to compose two similar alternative dialogues. They then perform the dialogues to the rest of the class, with appropriate acting. The dialogues may, of course, be slightly tongue-in-cheek: the abrupt one obviously aggressive, the polite one exaggeratedly deprecating.

Variations: To make it easier, you may prefer to compose the original (abrupt) dialogues yourself in advance, and give them to the groups directly – but this makes the exercise rather more mechanical and less creative.

When preparing their dialogues, the groups should decide on an exact context (setting and characters); then spectators may be asked to try to guess what these are.

```
BOX 51

                    Dialogue situations

 1 Getting someone to lend you some money.
 2 Selling flags for charity.
 3 Getting something to eat in a restaurant.
 4 Taking/giving in an assignment.
 5 Asking someone to give back something they've taken.
 6 Asking someone to go out with you.
 7 Getting help with lifting something heavy.
 8 Getting a noisy neighbour to be quiet.
 9 Helping a blind person to cross the road.
10 Asking the way.
11 Hitching a lift.
12 Booking a room in a hotel.
```

17.10 Then and now

Contrasting modals in past and present tenses, affirmative and negative
(e.g. *must/mustn't/don't have to/had to/didn't have to*); or *used to*
contrasted with present; written responses, with oral discussion follow-
up.

Procedure: Discuss with students how they remember their childhood
 – happier and freer than now? Or the opposite? Then ask them to write
 down four lists of differences between:
>   1 What they could do then, but can't (or mustn't) do now;
>   2 What they couldn't / weren't able to do then, but can now;
>   3 What they had to do then but don't have to do now;
>   4 What they didn't have to do then, but must now.

After ten or 15 minutes of writing (you may need to help with some
new vocabulary), ask them to read out some of the things they have; or
they may share their ideas in groups before reporting to the full class.
Finally, try to reach some overall conclusions; do these fit the impres-
sions given in the opening discussion?

Variations: The same exercise may be used to practise the quasi-modal
 used to: students can contrast what they used to do as young children
 with what they no longer do.

17.11 **Deductions**

Use of modals to express logical necessity or possibility (e.g. what *must/can't be true*, or *could have happened*); written and oral responses based on picture cues.

Materials: Ask as many students as possible to bring to class snapshots of people in their family. These should show the subject in the process of doing something – not static portraits. Bring a similar photograph of someone in your own family.

Procedure: Show your photograph, and ask the class to try to deduce whatever they can about its subject;

>   She must be your mother or sister – she looks like you!
>   That house might be in England.
>   That can't be you ... can it?

When they have exhausted their ideas, tell them the true background to the picture.

Then post their photographs round the class, with a sheet of paper under each one, and invite them to go round writing up their deductions or conjectures, using the same structures they have just used orally. Help individuals where necessary – and contribute your own ideas as well. Finally, read out the suggestions under each photograph, and ask its owner to give the true interpretation.

See also:
4.3   *Possible candidates;*
6.6   *Justifying actions;*
20.7   *Results of events;*
20.9   *By men, by women, or by both.*

18 Negative sentences

18.1 Erasing picture dictations

Negative sentences in the present based on picture cue; oral.

Procedure: Students dictate to you a simple picture – a scene, a person, a still-life – which you draw on the blackboard, adding new features as they suggest them (as in 16.3 *Picture dictation*). Then ask them to take the things you have drawn, in any order, and convey to you that they are **not** there, using simple negative sentences (these will often correspond to the affirmative sentences they used in the picture dictation). Whatever they negate in this way you have to erase. For example, they may have told you originally:

Alice has a feather on her hat.

but now someone may say:

Alice doesn't have a hat.

Whereupon you erase the hat (but may leave the feather hanging in the air!). This goes on until the board is empty.

18.2 Combining arrangement

Simple negative sentences in the present, contrasted with affirmative; oral interaction.

Materials: Two series of pictures of simple items (objects, animals or people), numbered, but displayed on separate pieces of paper. Items bearing the same number on each list should be similar, but may or may not correspond exactly. Where there are differences, these should be clear and easily expressed in simple language: a person with dark/fair hair, a dog sitting versus a dog standing, etc. There are some examples in *Box 52*; but you can easily make such materials yourself, using simple pictures (like those in *Box 5*, page 56, for example), altering where wished with correcting fluid or black pen, and photocopying.

Procedure: Students work in twos, each having one of the paired lists, which they are not allowed to show each other. Each student takes it in turn to describe or define an item, giving its number in the list, and the other student repeats the definition if it corresponds to his or her item with the same number, or contradicts it if not. The object is to find out if the items with the same number are identical or not. If the students decide they are, they put a tick next to them, if not, then a cross. Each pair of items may need several such exchanges in order to test if they really are the same or not. For example, the exchange about item one in the first pair of lists in *Box 52* might go as follows:

A: Number one is a man.

B: Yes, it's a man.

A: He has black hair.

B: No, he doesn't have black hair. (Both students mark number one with a cross.)

It is as well to do a brief full-class demonstration with one or two items before letting students work on their own. At the end, check that they have the ticks and crosses in the right places, and go through the definitions of the differences.

Comment: As with many group or pair work activities, it is worth having some other pairs of lists in reserve to give to students who finish early.

BOX 52

Combining arrangement worksheets

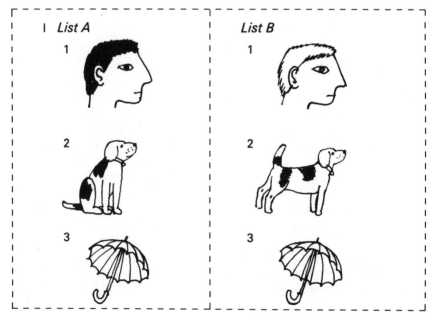

BOX 52   continued

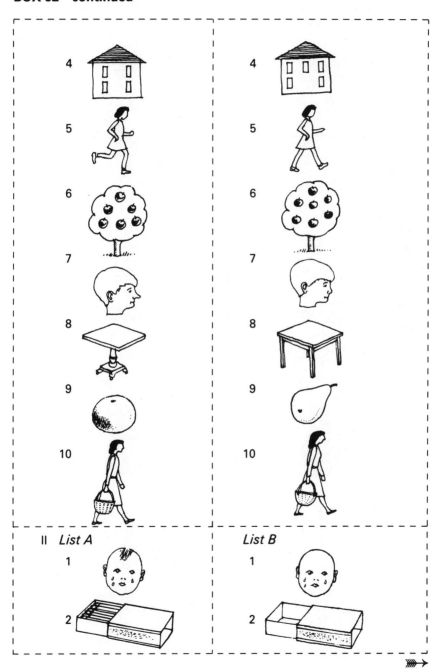

II *List A*   *List B*

BOX 52 continued

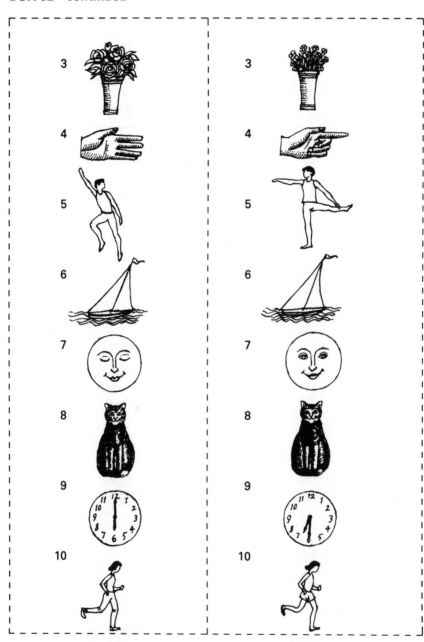

18.3 Picture differences

Simple negative sentences in the present, contrasted with affirmative; oral or written brainstorm, optional free interaction in pairs as follow-up.

Materials: Two or more pictures with ten or so minor differences between them that should be easily expressed in language the students know. You can use the pairs of pictures in *Box 53*, or several of those in *Box 49*, page 169.

BOX 53

Picture differences

Picture 1A

Picture 1B

⫸→

185

Procedure: Display the pictures, and ask students to find and define differences between them, using **negative** sentences; that is, they must define what is **not** so in one picture (contrasted with what **is** so in another). This is most easily done in a full-class oral brainstorm; but it may also be done individually in writing, with feedback later.

Variations: When students are familiar with this procedure, they may be divided into pairs, and each given a picture which they are not allowed to show one another. They have to discover the ten differences by question and answer, and write these down as negative sentences.

BOX 53 continued

Picture 2A

Picture 2B

BOX 53   continued

Picture 3A

Picture 3B

© Cambridge University Press 1988

Solutions to differences between pictures 1A and 1B.

1 In picture A the time is 3 o'clock, not 4 o'clock.
2 In picture A the notice doesn't say DEPARTURES, it says
   TIMETABLE.
3 In picture B the man in the foreground doesn't have a suitcase.
4 In picture B the man driving the truck has no hat.
5 In picture A the two people on the right aren't running, they are
   walking.

6 In picture B the doors on the left aren't open, they're shut.
7 In picture B the man in the foreground has no dog.
8 In picture B there is nobody sitting on the bench under the clock.
9 In picture A the gate to platform 3 isn't shut, it's open.
10 In picture B the little boy isn't looking at the notice, he's looking to the right.

Solutions to differences between pictures 2A and 2B.

1 In picture A there is no 'Car Park' sign.
2 In picture A the man standing by the road doesn't have fair hair; he has black hair.
3 In picture B the dog isn't sitting, it's standing.
4 In picture B the man on the other side of the road isn't running, he's walking.
5 In picture A the hand of the man telephoning isn't in his pocket.
6 In picture B there is no woman sitting in the car.
7 In picture B the man standing by the road doesn't have a tie.
8 In picture A the car isn't a taxi.
9 In picture B there is no word 'telephone' on the telephone box.
10 In picture B there is no postbox by the telephone.

Solution to differences between pictures 3A and 3B.

1 In picture A there are no birds in the sky.
2 In picture B there are no numbers on the number plate.
3 In picture B the man going into the shop doesn't have a briefcase.
4 In picture B the woman in the car isn't smiling.
5 In picture B the name of the filling station isn't DRAKE, it's BROOK.
6 In picture A, the man standing by the car doesn't have glasses.
7 In picture A there is no woman behind the cashtill in the shop.
8 In picture A the man filling the car isn't wearing a cap.
9 In picture B the big sign doesn't say TURN OFF ENGINE, only NO SMOKING.
10 In picture B there is no little boy in the back of the car.

18.4 Questionnaires with negative answers

Negative responses to set questions, contrasted with affirmative; oral or written.

Materials: Any type of questionnaire based on 'yes/no' questions (examples in *Boxes 40* and *43*, pages 144 and 153).

Procedure: Students administer the questionnaires to each other; positive answers may be given as 'yes', but negatives must be given in full sentences. If possible, each student should talk to several other students. Then ask for reports, in the third person, of negative replies that were given.

> Martine doesn't mind other people smoking near her.
>
> Jan doesn't enjoy smoking.

and try to reach some general conclusions:

> Most people don't like singing pop songs themselves.
>
> No one approves of smoking as a habit.

Or questionnaires may be done individually, in writing, and answers later shared and compared.

Variations: You may ask students to elicit both positive and negative answers equally, and discuss both kinds of response in your summing-up. There will be less concentrated practice of the negative forms, but the interaction will be easier and more natural, and negative forms when they occur will be better contextualized. You will also have better opportunities of contrasting these with affirmative forms.

18.5 Don't say no

Negative answers to questions; oral.

Procedure: One volunteer comes to the front of the class, and the others fire questions at him or her, trying to elicit the answer 'no'. The answerer must give true answers, but find alternative ways of denying or refusing; all answers must be in full sentences (answers like 'Not really', or 'Never' are unacceptable).

> A: Does the President of the United States live in Canada?
>
> B: The President of the United States does not live in Canada.
>
> C: Would you like to fail tomorrow's test?
>
> A: I would prefer not to fail tomorrow's test.

'Yes', however, is allowed; so students might slip in some 'yes' questions occasionally in order to lull the answerer's suspicions. When the answerer lets slip a 'no', or manages successfully to answer 20 questions without doing so, someone else takes their place.

18.6 Guessing without yes or no

Affirmative and negative answers to questions; brief oral responses.

Procedure: Half the class chooses an item to be guessed – and defines it as 'animal, vegetable or mineral'. For example, a diamond necklace is 'mineral', a cotton shirt is 'vegetable'. The other half of the class ask 'yes/no' questions to try to guess it. Any of the 'knowers' may answer, but they may not use the words 'yes' or 'no', only full-sentence confirmations or denials:

> A: Can we wear it?
>
> B: We can't wear it.

When the item has been guessed, the other half of the class chooses a new item to be guessed.

Comment: Most of the time the answers will tend to be negative, until a lot of possibilities have been eliminated and the 'guessers' are very near the right answer.

Note that there should be a number of 'knowers', not just one as in a conventional guessing procedure (see *Comment* to 15.6 *Guessing*). This is because they have rather more to do (full sentences rather than brief 'yes/no' responses) and in order to give more students opportunities to practise the negative.

18.7 Discrepancies

Negative sentences in any tense; oral responses, based on transformation of affirmative to negative; optional written follow-up.

Procedure: Improvise or read out a story to the students which has obvious inaccuracies or discrepancies in it. Every time they hear a mistake they put their hands up, tell you what is wrong, and give the correct version. You might take a well-known folk story or something they have just read from the coursebook.

> Teacher: Once upon a time there was a little girl called Goldi-
>   locks, who had long green hair...
>
> Student: Her hair wasn't green, it was golden...

Variations: You can base your spoken text on an inaccurate description of a picture (pictures in *Boxes 28, 39, and 53*, pages 106, 141, and 185 will do), or a picture of yourself, or of one of the students in the class. The text may be given in writing for homework; ask students to underline the erroneous bits in red, and write in corrections below: these should include what was wrong (usually a negative sentence) and what it should be (usually affirmative). Students welcome the opportunity to do some red-ink correction themselves!

See also:

16.5 *Reverse guessing* (using negative sentences as hints).

19 Numbers

19.1 Telephoning

Single cardinal numbers; listening comprehension, reading numbers.

Procedure: The object is for each student to find out the phone numbers of all the other members of the class. Each student notes down on a sheet of paper his or her own number (or invents a fictional one if they prefer, or don't have a phone). One student (or you) begins by announcing his or her own number, and ringing up someone else. And so on. It is a good idea to repeat each number at least twice.

> A: This is 06-933761, Mark speaking. This is 06-933761. Calling Pauline. Are you there Pauline?
>
> B: Yes, this is Pauline; my number is 04-224365. Pauline here at 04-224365...

Meanwhile all the students jot down the names of those who have identified themselves, with their corresponding numbers. At the end, check that all the numbers and names are right.

Variations: Make individual copies of a list of phone numbers – preferably the kinds of number combinations students are used to locally. There should be the same number of numbers on the list as there are students in the class. On each sheet a different number is underlined: this is the number of the student who has the sheet. The first student, after announcing his or her name and number calls another number, at random. The student whose number it is answers and calls another – and so on. All students note down numbers and corresponding names.

Comment: Note the need to teach specific telephone-linked expressions, such as the use of 'double-O' for '00', and conventional openings and closings of telephone conversations.

19.2 Address book

Simple cardinal numbers in addresses; listening comprehension and dictating.

Materials: In an earlier session, pass round a sheet and ask students to write down their names and addresses (and, if you wish, phone numbers) on it, very clearly. Add your own. Later, blank out all numbers with correcting fluid. Then make enough copies for each student to have one.

Procedure: Students fill in the missing numbers in their own addresses, and any others they happen to know. They then go round – in pairs, rather than individually – finding out from each other, and you, all the numbers that they lack. When the first students finish, stop the activity. Read out all the complete addresses yourself, in order to check that everyone has them right, and to give people who didn't finish a chance to fill gaps. At the end, they have an address list for keeping in touch with each other.

19.3 Number dictation (1)

Larger cardinal numbers: listening comprehension.

Procedure: Dictate a series of numbers in the hundreds, in random order, writing them down yourself as you do so. Go on to the next number as soon as the last student has finished writing. How many did the class get through in two minutes? Check answers, and then do it again with another series of numbers; the class tries to break its 'record' for the two minutes.

Variations: To make it easier, use numbers between ten and a hundred; to make it more difficult, go up to the thousands or higher.

19.4 Number dictation (2)

Larger cardinal numbers; listening comprehension and dictating.

Procedure: The first student dictates a number (in the hundreds) to the class; everyone writes it down. The second dictates another number, which everyone writes down, and adds to the first. As each new number is given, it is noted down and added to the previous total. Has everyone reached the same grand total at the end? If pocket calculators are available, use them.

Variations: This can be conveniently done in groups of not less than five students.

You can, of course, use bigger numbers, or include 'minus' numbers, or decimal points, or fractions, if you wish to make the activity more challenging.

19.5 Numbers that are important to me

Any numbers, particularly as used in dates: oral interaction.

Procedure: Ask the students to write down:
    1 A year that was important in their lives (e.g. 1980).
    2 A date that is/was important to them (e.g. January 12th).
    3 A telephone number that is/was important to them.
    4 Any other number that has special personal significance.
One (volunteer) student reads out his or her numbers; other students guess what the significance of the numbers might be; the student tells them what in fact this is. Then the class divides into groups, and the papers with the numbers on are displayed to all members of the group; participants discuss the different numbers and their background 'stories'.

Comment: Note that this kind of activity demands a certain intimacy and frankness, and should only be attempted in a class where relationships are warm and informal. Also, students should not have to reveal the background of all their numbers if they do not want to: let them choose which they would like to talk about.

19.6 Exam results

Ordinal numbers; simple utterances based on number cues.

Materials: Five separate sheets, each giving information on the results of four (out of 20) candidates in exams in three subjects. These results are given as placings, not marks. For example, '2 Reg' means that Reg came second. Examples in *Box 54*.

Procedure: Students sit in groups of five, each participant having one of the sheets. They are not allowed to show each other their sheets, but have to fill in the missing information by asking each other questions:
    Who came fourth in English?
or simply by dictating their information to each other:
    Reg came ninth in English, second in maths, and sixth in art.

Variations: The groups might work out the average placing of each candidate in a final list – and compare results with one another.

》》→

BOX 54

Exam results

List 1

English	Maths	Maths
1	1	1 Dick
2	2	2
3 Ann	3 Beth	3 Chad
4	4	4
5	5	5
6	6	6
7 Beth	7	7
8	8 Ann	8
9	9	9
10	10 Dick	10
11	11 Chad	11
12	12	12 Ann
13 Chad	13	13 Beth
14	14	14
15	15	15
16	16	16
17 Dick	17	17
18	18	18
19	19	19
20	20	20

List 2

English	Maths	Art
1	1	1
2	2	2
3	3	3
4	4 Eva	4 Fred
5 Gary	5	5 Eva
6	6	6
7	7	7
8	8	8 Gary
9	9	9
10	10	10
11 Eva	11	11
12	12	12
13	13 Hedy	13
14	14	14 Hedy
15 Hedy	15	15
16	16 Fred	16
17	17	17
18	18	18
19	19 Gary	19
20 Fred	20	20

List 3

English	Maths	Art
1	1	1
2 Jill	2	2
3	3	3
4	4	4
5	5	5
6 Ian	6 Jill	6
7	7 Kate	7
8	8	8
9	9 Ian	9 Leah
10	10	10
11	11	11
12	12	12
13	13	13
14	14 Leah	14
15	15	15
16 Leah	16	16
17	17	17
18	18	18 Kate
19 Kate	19	19 Jill
20	20	20 Ian

List 4

English	Maths	Art
1 Ned	1 Meg	1
2	2	2 Meg
3	3	3
4 Meg	4	4
5	5 Ned	5
6	6	6
7	7	7 Ned
8 Ora	8	8
9	9	9
10 Pat	10	10
11	11	11
12	12	12
13	13	13
14	14	14
15	15 Pat	15
16	16	16 Pat
17	17	17 Ora
18	18	18
19	19	19
20	20 Ora	20

BOX 54   continued

List 5				Solution		
English	*Maths*	*Art*		*English*	*Maths*	*Art*
1	1	1		1 Ned	1 Meg	1 Dick
2	2 Reg	2		2 Jill	2 Reg	2 Meg
3	3	3		3 Ann	3 Beth	3 Chad
4	4	4		4 Meg	4 Eva	4 Fred
5	5	5		5 Gary	5 Ned	5 Eva
6	6	6 Reg		6 Ian	6 Jill	6 Reg
7	7	7		7 Beth	7 Kate	7 Ned
8	8	8		8 Ora	8 Ann	8 Gary
9 Reg	9	9		9 Reg	9 Ian	9 Leah
10	10	10 Stan		10 Pat	10 Dick	10 Stan
11	11	11 Vera		11 Eva	11 Chad	11 Vera
12 Tony	12 Vera	12		12 Tony	12 Vera	12 Ann
13	13	13		13 Chad	13 Hedy	13 Beth
14 Vera	14	14		14 Vera	14 Leah	14 Hedy
15	15	15 Tony		15 Hedy	15 Pat	15 Tony
16	16	16		16 Leah	16 Fred	16 Pat
17	17 Stan	17		17 Dick	17 Stan	17 Ora
18 Stan	18 Tony	18		18 Stan	18 Tony	18 Kate
19	19	19		19 Kate	19 Gary	19 Jill
20	20	20		20 Fred	20 Ora	20 Ian

© Cambridge University Press 1988

19.7   Getting in order

Ordinal numbers; free discussion.

Procedure: Put students in a line; then ask them to rearrange themselves according to the dates of their birthdays – the one nearest to the first of January at one end, the one nearest to the 31st of December at the other. Each one should find out which number he or she is within the class – third? tenth? sixteenth? Then put them into groups of five to ten students and ask them to find as many other ways of ranking themselves in order as they can. For example: in 'length of name', Jacqueline is first, Penelope and Jonathan second, Robin fourth, Kate fifth and Ian sixth; but in 'distance we travel each morning to get here', the order might be quite different. Then the groups tell each other some of their more original ideas for rankings – and the order they put themselves in.

⟫→

195

Variations: Groups try to find different reasons for ranking that will give each participant at least one opportunity to be in first place.

Groups might simply recount one of the orders that they have found, and challenge other groups to guess the rationale behind it.

Jacqueline is first, Penelope and Jonathan second, Robin fourth, Kate fifth and Ian sixth: what are they in order of?

But obviously this will work only if the necessary background information is likely to be known by all.

See also:
8.3 *Kim's game (Variation).*

20 Passives

20.1 Passives in the press

Passive sentences, all tenses; reading and understanding, expanding brief headlines; writing.

Materials: A pile of English-language newspapers.

Procedure: Give each student a newspaper, and ask them to go through the headlines and news reports, highlighting or underlining occurrences of passive constructions, and using dictionaries where necessary to understand the meaning. If the passives occur abbreviated in headlines, they should expand them into proper sentences in their notebooks. For example:

Man struck by lightning in wood

becomes:

A man has been struck by lightning in a wood.

(Often the first sentence or two of the article will give some indication of what the expanded headline should look like.) After 15 or so minutes of such activity – during which you can help individuals with difficulties in comprehension – stop them, and ask to hear some of the items they have found.

Comment: Some of the items will probably stimulate discussion; a good thing, up to a point, but don't let them get you away from the main point of the exercise for too long!

You may need to teach a little 'journalese' when working on headlines: the use of infinitives to indicate the future passive ('Forest to be cut down'), and the use of short or abbreviated words for more usual long ones ('Demo banned'). In such cases, you may wish to encourage them to change vocabulary as well as expand grammatical forms.

20.2 What is done – and by whom?

Present passive sentences, with agent; oral and written brainstorm.

Procedure: Give the students the name of an institution or centre of activity that they know of – the school, a sports centre, the local government offices, a theatre, a street, a hotel, an airport – and ask them to list all the things that *are* normally *done* at this location. Write up their suggestions on the board. In a hotel, for example, they might say:

> Credit cards are accepted.
> Food is eaten.
> Meals are served.
> Guests are welcomed.

Then ask them to identify **by whom** these things are done. Each student writes down the name of an agent suitable to each sentence (you may need to supply some new vocabulary here); then compare and discuss. For example – by whom are credit cards accepted? By the receptionist? Or by the hotel management?

Variations: Erase or hide what has been written. Can they remember and write down the things that are done by ... the receptionist? The guests? The waiters?

20.3 Describing changes

Passive sentences in various tenses; oral brainstorm; optionally, the structure *need*(s) *doing/to be done.*

Materials: Pairs of pictures showing a situation or place before and after a set of changes – like those in *Box 55*, for example.

Procedure: Ask the students to imagine that the second picture is the present and to describe what *has been done.* Or let them assume that the first is the present, and describe what they know *will be done* (i.e. the second picture). Or they can imagine that they are midway between the two, and describe what is in the process of *being done* in order for the situation in the first picture to change into the second. This can be done orally or in writing.

Variations: Showing only the first picture of one of the pairs in *Box 55*, ask students to guess what changes *will be made* – or, in the case of the untidy room, *need to be made.* Write up all suggestions, then look at the second picture: how much did they get right? What did they miss?

Discuss the local situation: changes that *have been made* over the last few years, things that *are going to be done* in the future. Ask students to tell you the changes that seem to them to be for the worse, or for the better. Or what they think *needs to be done* or *needs doing* – will it in fact *be done?*

BOX 55

Pictures showing changes

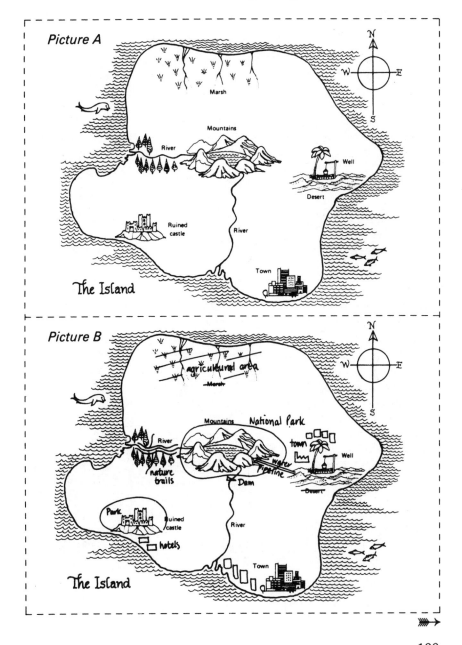

BOX 55   continued

Picture A

Picture B

BOX 55 continued

Picture A

Picture B

20.4 Writing up a process

Use of present simple passive for formal description of process; written composition.

Procedure: Discuss with the class how you would describe a process involving a series of operations – such as a physics experiment – using the present simple passive, and write up such a description with them:

> The equipment is set up ...
> A litre of water is heated ...

Then ask each student to choose one such process he or she is familiar with – but perhaps the others are not – and describe it similarly. You may need to supply some new vocabulary, as individuals request it. After writing out their descriptions, students get together in pairs to teach each other about 'their' processes, and to check the quality of their own explanations. Are these clear enough to be followed by a layman? When you have checked their descriptions, the more interesting ones can be read out.

Comment: Note that the passive is not appropriate for the description of everyday domestic processes (washing, cooking, etc.), but rather for scientific experiments and technical operations. Hence this activity is most suitable for ESP or EST classes, using ideas drawn from their main subjects.

20.5 What's being done?

Use of present progressive passive to describe a process going on at the time of speaking; brainstorm, oral and written.

Procedure: Suggest a few things that *are being done* at the present moment within, say, a kilometre radius of the classroom:

> The road is being mended.
> Cars are being driven.

then divide the class into groups, and ask each group to list as many different such activities as they can in five minutes. Which group has the most ideas?

20.6 Election campaign

Use of future passive to express promises: free composition of sentences, oral and written.

Procedure: Tell the students they are preparing part of a candidate's campaign for election to a post in either national or local government. What sort of things should their candidate promise in order to gain votes: what should he or she undertake *will be done?* For example:

The main road in this town will be widened.

A new school will be built.

More jobs will be provided for young school-leavers.

Elicit a few such suggestions from the class and write them on the board. Then divide the class into groups, each of which is supporting a different candidate: they work out a programme of what *will be done* if their candidate is elected, and write it out. Supply new vocabulary as asked for, and write it on the board.

Then the 'candidates' (role-played by one member of each group) present their programmes, supported and prompted if necessary by members of the groups. Finally, one of the candidates may be selected by the class in a democratic election (participants are not allowed to vote for 'their' candidates).

20.7 Results of events

Past or future passive: free composition of sentences, oral or written.

Procedure: Describe briefly an event which would be likely to have far-reaching consequences: an unusually heavy rainstorm; a sudden rise in the birthrate; a flu epidemic. Write a sentence describing the event in the centre of the board, in the past tense, and ask the class to suggest what they imagine *was done* by the authorities to cope with it – and any other consequences that can be expressed as passives. Results – and results-of-results – are written up as a flow-chart. Thus the sentence:

An unusually large
number of
babies were born.

may lead to:

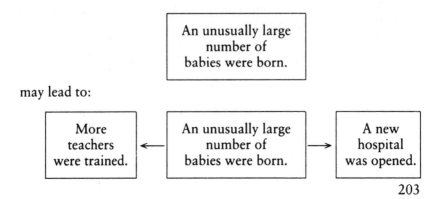

| More teachers were trained. | ← | An unusually large number of babies were born. | → | A new hospital was opened. |

which in turn may lead to:

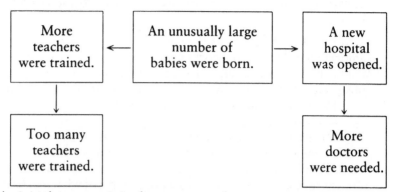

If the initial sentence is in the present perfect:

An unusually large number of babies has been born.

then the following passive sentences will be in the future:

A new hospital will be opened.

and will represent estimations of what will be done as a consequence, rather than events assumed to have taken place already. Some more ideas for initial events, not marked for tense, are shown in *Box 56.*

Variations: You may wish to use genuine historical events with interesting consequences, or events connected with other subjects the students are studying.

The activity may be done in small groups; give each group a large sheet of paper with the initial event written in the middle, appoint a 'secretary' and ask them to suggest things done in consequence and draw in the flow-chart. After you have checked, display the results.

20.8 Defining objects

Present passive with modals (e.g. *It can be done*); oral brainstorm.

Procedure: Choose a simple inanimate object, and tell all the class but one what it is. Students describe it by saying what *can be done* (or *must/should be done*) with it, until the one who does not know can guess. For example, an egg might be described by sentences like:

It can be eaten.
It must be eaten fresh.
It can be broken.

The guesser may also ask questions:

Can it be boiled?
Can it be decorated?

BOX 56

Events with far-reaching results

A   Worldwide

    1 A cure found for cancer
    2 Return of the ice age
    3 Explosion of Bomb
    4 Sudden rise in birthrate
    5 Invasion from outer space

B   National

    1 War declared by neighbouring country
    2 Large amounts of oil discovered offshore
    3 Sudden fall in industrial production
    4 Celebration of national jubilee
    5 Doctors on strike

C   Local

    1 Collapse of hotel in centre of town
    2 Heavy rainstorms
    3 New motorway
    4 Olympic Games held here
    5 Flu epidemic

20.9   By men, by women, or by both

Present simple passive with agent; brainstorm, oral and written; discussion follow-up using modals *should, can, might* with passive.

Procedure: Ask students to write down five things that are normally, or more usually, done by men, five that are normally done by women, and five that are normally done equally by both – excluding obvious biological functions! (Tell them to consider what the situation really **is** in a society with which they are familiar– not what they think it **should,** be!) In groups or in full class, share ideas: do they agree with each other?

Variations: Whittle down the list to things that the students more or less agree are usually done by one of the sexes rather than the other. Then ask them whether they think such situations are justified. Take in turn each activity listed, and discuss whether it *can/might/should be done* by a member of the opposite sex – and what the implications are if it is.

21 Past perfect

21.1 Past diary

Use of past perfect to describe events done by a certain time in the past; construction of simple sentences based on set cues; oral or written.

Materials: A diary of daily events, such as those in *Boxes 25* and *27a*, pages 96 and 102; individual copies, or shown on overhead projector.

Procedure: Present the diary as representing the events of last week; the writer is called Mickey. Pick one day; ask the class what Mickey *had done* by three o'clock of that day. Then ask them to look carefully at the schedules of two days (say, Tuesday and Wednesday). Then, without looking, they should try to write down as much as they can remember of what Mickey *had done* by, say, one o'clock on Wednesday, and what he or she had *not yet done*. Check: have they, between them, remembered everything?

21.2 Changes: before and after

Past perfect contrasted with past simple; construction of written sentences based on set pattern, followed by free oral interaction and writing.

Procedure: Ask each student to think of some period that made a great impression on him or her: a course of study, an impressive trip, some kind of edifying (or traumatic!) experience. Then ask them to express the difference it made to them in a sentence, or sentences, based on the formula:

I had never (or always) ... before.

and possibly adding:

But afterwards I ...

using the past perfect in the first clause and the past simple in the second. Give an example yourself, from your own life. Then ask students to write down their sentences – as many as possible, to express the widest possible implications of their experiences. Supply vocabulary to individuals as needed.

Then ask a volunteer student to describe his or her experience, and to explain to the class what differences it made to his or her life – using the written sentences as a basis, but amplifying freely.

Variations: Students may tell their experiences to one another in pairs – and then report back to the class in the third person, each student describing the experiences of his or her partner.

The same may be done in writing, preferably as follow-up to the oral activity. Ask the students to describe the difference something made to their lives, contrasting what they had been/known/felt beforehand with their situation afterwards.

See also:
6.7   *Looking back*;
13.2   *Reporting interviews*;
22.2   *What were you doing last night?* (2);
26.6   *Accounting for moods* (assuming the mood was in the past).

22 Past progressive

22.1 What were you doing last night? (1)

Use of past progressive to describe past period of activity; composition of simple sentences based on picture cues; oral with written follow-up.

Materials: A set of pictures of simple objects, as in *Box 5*, page 56.

Procedure: Each student gets a picture and decides what he or she was doing (in imagination) at a given time last night – say, at ten o'clock: the activity must involve the item depicted. Then each student shows his or her picture and says what he or she was doing. A student with a picture of a vase might say:

I was putting flowers in a vase.

One with a picture of a loaf of bread might say:

I was making sandwiches.

The students then have to find companions. They go round asking each other:

What were you doing last night?

If two or more students find that they were doing activities that could 'go together', they join up. For example, someone who was making sandwiches and someone putting flowers in a vase could go together: they might have been preparing for a party. When most of the students are in groups of three or more, they report back to the full class: what each one was doing, and what the 'umbrella' activity was that accounted for their being together (e.g. they were preparing for a party). Can the class find a group for any students who have not managed to find one for themselves?

22.2 What were you doing last night? (2)

Use of past progressive to describe past period of activity; composition of simple sentences based on picture cues.

Materials: A set of pictures of simple objects, as in *Box 5*, page 56.

Procedure: This begins the same way as the previous activity. Each student gets a picture, and decides what he or she *was doing* last night, involving the item depicted. But the activity must **not** be an obvious

208

one. For example, someone who has a vase should not say:

> I was putting flowers in a vase.

but something unexpected, like:

> I was drinking wine out of my vase.
> I was selling my vase to a friend for $2,000.

You may need to supply some new vocabulary.

Then each student says what he or she was doing, and justifies it, possibly using the past perfect:

> I was drinking wine out of my vase because I had broken all my glasses.
> I was selling my vase for $2,000 because I had discovered it was made of gold.

Variations: Gather in the pictures and stick them up on the board with blu-tack. Point to each in turn – can the students (not the one whose picture it was!) recall who was doing what with it?

22.3 Are you a good witness?

Use of past progressive to describe given past situation; free composition of sentences based on picture cue; oral and written.

Materials: A picture depicting a large number of things going on – a scene in a street, for example, or in an airport terminal, or in the living-room of a large family. Examples in *Box 57*; or use published materials (see BIBLIOGRAPHY); or you may find suitable pictures in your coursebook. Choose pictures whose topics are within the scope of your students' vocabulary.

Procedure: Tell the students you are going to give them a test to see if they are good witnesses or not. They will have to look at a scene and then recall details in response to questions. Show them the picture for two minutes, then hide it and give them a series of questions to test their perception and memory:

> Which way was the old woman facing – left or right?
> Was the baby wearing a hat?

You can improvise these, and get immediate volunteered responses; or prepare them in written form in advance – in which case the students write down their answers (in complete sentences) to be checked later.

See if the class can establish who the best witnesses are!

Variations: In a more demanding version, students are asked to write down everything they can remember that was going on in the scene. Or they can work in groups, pooling their knowledge and composing a written account together.

The students themselves may provide the original material for

BOX 57

Things going on

recalling, by setting up a living tableau. Groups prepare more or less dramatic tableaux, hold them stationary for a minute or two – and then challenge the other students to recall what was going on.

22.4 When did we meet?

Past progressive to refer to things going on at certain times in the past; optionally, contrast with past simple; expanding notes into full sentences; oral interaction.

Materials: Four lists of activity schedules, describing a certain day in the lives of four different people; optionally, a map showing the places referred to. My sample texts in *Box 58* go with the map of the 'developed' island (*Box 55*, page 199).

Procedure: Put the students in groups of four, each participant having one of the lists and a copy of the map. Take one or two examples of items on the lists, and show the full class how they may be expanded in speech. For example:

Lunch   13.00–14.00

might be said as:

I was having lunch from one o'clock to two o'clock.

You might ask your students to use only the past progressive; or, if they have grasped the contrast, to use the past simple occasionally to refer to specific events or to a sequence:

I came back to the hotel at half past one.

I got up and then had breakfast.

Tell students that each of the four met each of the others in the course of the day. They have to find out when and where. Each of them in turn should recount what they did (using sentences like the above examples), while the others listen and try to identify when/where they must have met. After everyone has described their day, they may need to ask each other questions, which may use either the past simple or the past progressive:

What time did you leave the Nature Reserve?

What were you doing at six o'clock / between four and six?

At the end, each participant prepares a note stating where he or she met each of the others, and what he or she, and the other person, were doing at the time. Compare and check results.

≫→

See also:
23.7 *Story behind a photo.*

BOX 58

Day schedules of four people

A
(Staying at Grand Hotel)

Get up 9.00
Breakfast in hotel 9.00–9.30
Visit Castle museum 9.30–11.30
Swim in sea 11.30–13.30
Back to hotel 13.30
Lunch, rest at hotel 13.30–16.00
Tea at hotel 16.00–16.30
Leave hotel 16.30
Walk, Castle beach 16.30–18.30
Back to hotel 18.30
Shower and change 18.30–19.30
Dinner at hotel 19.30–21.00
Party at hotel 21.00–23.30
Bed 23.30

B
(Staying in tent, Castle Beach camp)

Get up 7.00
Swim in sea 7.00–8.00
Back to camp 8.00
Breakfast 8.00–9.00
Walk to Nature Reserve 9.00–13.00
Reach Nature Reserve 13.00
Picnic lunch by river 13.00–14.00
Fish in river 14.00–17.00
Tea at Nature Reserve Cafe 17.00
Hitch lift to Castle beach
    17.00–18.00
Walk to camp via beach
    18.00–19.00
Supper at camp 19.00–20.30
Sing-song at camp 20.30–22.00
Bed 22.00

C
(Lives in town)

Get up 7.30
Breakfast at home 8.00–8.30
Drive to north coast 8.30–11.00
Survey area 11.00–14.00
Eat sandwiches in car 14.00
Continue survey 14.00–16.00
Drive south via Nature Reserve
    16.00–18.00
Arrive Castle 18.00
Make phone calls, hotel
    18.00–18.30
Dinner at hotel 18.30–20.00
Leave hotel 20.30
Drive home 20.30–21.00
Television 21.00–23.30
Bed 23.30

D
(Living on yacht)

Reach north coast of island 4.00
Sleep 4.00–10.00
Breakfast 10.00–10.30
Land 10.30
Explore coast on foot
    10.30–12.30
Back to yacht 12.30
Sail round west coast 12.30–15.00
Go up river (motorboat)
    15.00–16.30
Go back down river 16.30–17.30
Back to yacht 17.30
Sail south, to Castle 17.30–20.30
Eat, shower, change 20.30–22.00
Go to hotel party 22.00–24.00
Back to yacht, bed, 24.00

© Cambridge University Press 1988

23 Past simple

23.1 Listening to stories

Use of past for narrative; listening comprehension and slot-filling; oral.

Procedure: Tell the students a story – improvising from skeleton notes, or reading out from a text (see BIBLIOGRAPHY for recommended sources). The story should have plenty of action, and be easily comprehensible to the students. Get them to focus on past forms by asking occasionally for a translation of an irregular form, or by stopping and getting them to supply the verb – but not so often as to interfere with overall 'pace' or comprehensibility. After you have finished, ask them to recall some of the sentences in the past that were mentioned in the story – using one-word 'cues' to jog their memories.

Comment: You do not have to finish a single story in one session; use longer stories, or complete books, and read them in serial form, a few minutes each lesson.

23.2 Piling up events

Use of past for narrative; repetition and construction of simple sentences based on given past forms; oral, with optional written follow-up.

Procedure: Give each student a verb in the past tense ('sat' or 'stood' or 'gave'). Then start a simple chain of events with the sentence:
> Yesterday I went to town and I bought a loaf of bread ...

The first student continues, repeating your sentence but adding a further clause including his or her verb:
> Yesterday I went to town, I bought a loaf of bread and I *sat* on a park bench ...

The second continues likewise:
> Yesterday, I went to town, I bought a loaf of bread, I sat on a park bench, and I *stood* at the bus stop ...

And so on, until all the students have contributed, or until the chain becomes impossible to remember.

Variations: Immediately after finishing the above procedure, ask students to write down as much as they can recall of the final chain – possibly working in pairs or groups to help each other remember.

Instead of giving verbs in the past tense, give them in the 'base' form, so that they have to supply the past form themselves. Or simply let them choose their own – either in advance, or on the spur of the moment.

23.3 Chain story

Use of past for narrative; composition of sentences based on given past forms; oral, with optional written follow-up.

Procedure: Give each student a single past form ('thought' or 'spoke' or 'went'). Begin improvising a story – for example:

> Once upon a time there was a very old fisherman who lived in a cave near the sea. Every day he went out in his little boat to catch fish. One day there was a terrible storm...

When you stop, a student has to continue, bringing his or her past form into the story. For example, if it was 'thought', he or she might say:

> ... and he could not go out to sea in his little boat. 'What can I do?' he *thought*, 'if I don't catch any fish, I won't have any money, or any food...'

And on to the next student, until all have contributed, and all past forms have been woven in. Unlike the previous activity, students do not have to repeat what the one before them has said, and their contributions can be much longer and more elaborate.

Variations: Students may be given simple base forms of the verb, and derive the past forms themselves for putting into their 'instalments'. Or they may get (or choose themselves) other kinds of words, not necessarily past forms – a good way of practising recently-learnt vocabulary. Or they may be given pictures which they have to use as illustrations to their contributions.

You may wish to write the whole story on the board. This slows things down, but focuses attention on correct forms, and adds the written dimension.

The original graphic or written cues can be used after the end of the narration to stimulate recall of the various contributions:

> Who remembers what bit of the story included the word *thought*?
> Who remembers what happened at this picture?

– a memory test which also provides extra review of the material.

The same activity can be done in class in writing. Each student prepares a personal list of about 15 verbs, and keeps it by him or her throughout the activity. On a separate piece of paper each student writes the opening sentence of a story, using the first verb on his or her list; and then passes the paper to a neighbour. On the papers they have just received, students write a continuation of the story (one sentence), using the second verb on their list – and so on, until all the verbs are used up. Stories are then read out.

23.4 Pictures into story

Use of past for narrative; free composition of stories based on picture cues; oral or written.

Materials: Simple picture stories, like those in *Box 59*, shown on overhead projector or distributed to individual students. You will probably find similar material in your coursebook.

Procedure: Taking the pictures one by one, ask students to narrate, orally or in writing, the story they show. They should do this in as much detail as possible. They are not, of course, limited to the events actually depicted; encourage them to use their own imaginations to fill in background information, dialogue, character analysis and so on. Supply new vocabulary as needed.

Variations: Display only the first picture, get the students to start telling the story, and then let them brainstorm ideas as to what happened next. Show them the next picture, let them describe the events it shows (were their guesses right?), and continue similarly with the later pictures.

》》》→

BOX 59

Picture stories

1

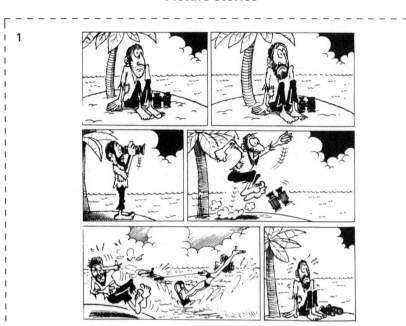

2

BOX 59   continued

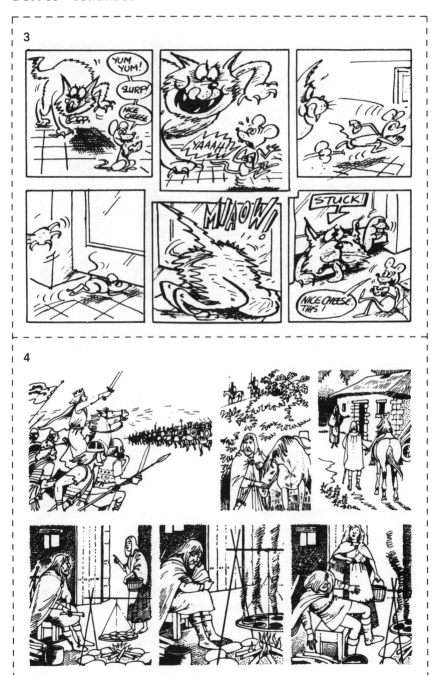

BOX 59   continued

© Cambridge University Press

23.5   Putting stories in order

Use of past for narrative; free composition of sentences based on picture cues; oral or written.

Materials: Sets of pictures apparently showing story – but ambiguous: could be taken in any order (*Box 60*).

Procedure: After the students have had some practice working from picture stories, as in 23.4 *Pictures into story* above, put them into groups and give each group a set of the pictures – each picture on a separate piece of paper. The groups then decide in what order they want their pictures to be, and write an appropriate story. If a group finishes early, it puts the pictures in another order and writes another story.

Each group in turn then reads out a story they have written. As they do so, other groups arrange the pictures in the order they think the story implies; check they all have the right order before going on to the next story.

Variations: Is there a 'best' or 'most probable' order of the pictures? Discuss.

For homework, give students another set of similar pictures to write a story about.

BOX 60

Ambiguous picture stories

BOX 60 continued

3

23.6   Changes in one's life

Use of past to describe personal experiences; free composition of sentences, oral and written; discussion.

Procedure: Ask the students to think of an event in their life that made a big difference to them. Start the ball rolling by describing a change in your own life; encourage them to ask you questions about it. Then ask for a student volunteer to describe a similar experience, helping with vocabulary where needed. Other students contribute further, until the class has had enough. Then ask them all to write down descriptions of their 'change' experiences for homework. If you wish, and if your students agree, some of the resulting essays can be read out later.

23.7   Story behind a photo

Use of past for narrative; also past interrogative; free discussion, with written composition follow-up.

Materials: In a previous session ask the students to bring to the classroom photographs of themselves, or someone they know, taken some time ago; and bring one yourself.
Procedure: Show the students your photograph, and tell them about the circumstances in which it was taken, or any other interesting facts (in the past) connected with it. Encourage them to ask questions. Then invite another student to display his or her photograph and talk about it. And so on, round the class.
Variations: The activity may be based on questions, in the past, about the photograph. The owner of the photograph simply states who the subject is – and from then on all information is given in answer to questions:
>   Where was this taken?
>   Did you live there long?
For homework, ask students to write a brief composition based on a similar photograph.

23.8   What really happened?

Use of past for narrative; reading out and understanding short sentences, followed by discussion.

Materials: Four grids, each giving partial information about a sequence of events involving four characters and certain times, as in *Box 61.* I

⫸→ *p. 224*

BOX 61

Story in four grids

Grid A

	January – June 1986	July – December 1986	January – June 1987	July – December 1987
Alex	Met Don in Chicago, February			
Myra			Paid $2m into New York bank, March	
Don				Was arrested in Paris, September
Ken		Talked to Myra in restaurant, New York, September		

Grid B

	January– June 1986	July– December 1986	January– June 1987	July– December 1987
Alex				Threw himself under a train in London, August
Myra		Had baby, London, November		
Don	Paid Alex $10m, Chicago, March			
Ken			Was at Don's wedding, London, May	

BOX 61   continued

Grid C

	January – June 1986	July – December 1986	January – June 1987	July – December 1987
Alex		Paid Myra $1m, New York, August		
Myra	Stayed in Chicago hotel, January–June			
Don			Married Myra, London, May	
Ken				Adopted Myra's baby, Paris, December

Grid D

	January – June 1986	July – December 1986	January – June 1987	July – December 1987
Alex			Met Myra, New York, March	
Myra				Fell from high building died, London, July
Don		Met Myra, London, December		
Ken	Saw Don with Alex, Chicago, February			

know of no similar published materials; but these are quite easy – and fun – to construct yourself in a spare hour.

Procedure: Put the class into groups of four, each group participant having one of the four grids. Without showing their papers to one another, they exchange necessary information to fill all the spaces in all the grids:

> Alex met Myra in New York in March, 1987.
> What did Myra do in the first half of 1986?

(You may need to start off with all the class together, showing them how to fill in one or two of the spaces. However, if they are used to information-gap group work this will not be necessary.)

Then ask the groups or individuals to try to reconstruct the story behind the events given: Why did Don pay Alex all that money? Was Myra's death an accident? And so on. They should write out their finished thrillers for presentation to the class at the end.

23.9   Sounds interesting

Use of past for narrating; free composition of story, based on sound cues.

Materials: A recorded series of sounds, lasting two minutes or so. You can make these yourself, or use published materials (see BIBLIOGRAPHY).

Procedure: Tell the class a recording has been found of a sequence of events – but no one knows what really happened. Can they, by listening to the recorded sounds, reconstruct the story? Let them listen to the sounds two or three times, noting down ideas; then they should get together in pairs or small groups and try to reconstruct the story. They may want to hear the recording again once or twice as they are working, and will probably need help with vocabulary. Finally, let them read out suggestions.

Comment: You should prepare a suggested interpretation of your own to contribute: it is interesting to compare your ideas with those of the students.

23.10   Alibi

Questions in the past; oral interaction.

Procedure: Select a scene and time for a crime – say, a bank robbery, at a well-known bank in the middle of town, at 11 o'clock yesterday. Two students are the 'suspects' – they are sent outside and instructed to prepare an 'alibi' for one another. This means they have to invent and be prepared to describe a situation during the period of the crime, in which they were in each other's company and can therefore vouch for each other's innocence. For example, they were shopping in a different part of town, or cycling together in the country. The class, who are the 'detectives', prepare a number of questions to ask them:

> Where exactly were you?
> What did you buy there?
> How much did it cost?

and so on. Meanwhile the 'suspects' prepare their story to try to anticipate all such questions and give exactly corresponding versions of their alibi. After about five minutes of preparation, the first suspect is called in and asked questions about his or her movements and actions during the crucial time. Then the second. If they do in fact corroborate each other's stories, they are 'innocent'; but if there are inconsistencies and contradictions, they are 'guilty'.

23.11 Cooperative story

Use of past for narrative: free written composition.

Procedure: Give each student a large blank sheet of paper, and the title of a story, which should include the names of a hero and heroine – say *Cliff and Sabrina*. Each student writes the title and the first sentence of the story, and passes the paper to a neighbour. The neighbour writes the next sentence in the story, and folds the paper over to hide the title and first sentence, leaving only his or her own sentence exposed; so the next student to get the story will only see the last sentence. And so on, each student contributing a sentence and folding the paper over to hide what went before, before passing it on.

   When you (or the class) have had enough, or the papers are full, open them up and read out the resulting stories.

Variations: For less entertaining results but perhaps more satisfying writing, let the students leave the papers open the whole time; then each student adds his or her contribution on the basis of everything that has gone before.

   For homework, ask students to write the story that they would have composed on the basis of their own opening sentence.

See also:

24 Possessives

(including possessive *'s* and possessive adjectives and pronouns)

24.1 Detectives

The possessive pronouns *mine, yours, his, hers*; oral production of set dialogue.

Procedure: Send one student (the 'detective') outside, and ask another student for something that belongs to him or her, but is not easily identifiable – a pencil, a standard textbook, etc. The detective comes back, is given the object, and asks one of the students:

Is this yours?

The student – whether it is in fact his or hers or not – denies it:

No, it isn't mine. It's his. (indicating another student)

The detective then asks the student indicated, and so on round the class; at the end, he or she has to try to identify who in fact was lying and is the owner of the object.

24.2 Family tree

Use of possessive *'s* to indicate relationships; composition of simple sentences based on family-tree diagram; oral or written.

Materials: A diagram of a family tree, presented on the board or overhead projector. The family tree may be an invented one, like those in *Box 62* (or you may find one in your coursebook); or, better, a representation of a family the class know of and can relate to: your own, one of theirs, the British royal family, a television soap-opera family.

Procedure: Ask students to define the relationship between any two of the names, using the possessive *'s*:

John is Fay's husband.

Jack is Tom's uncle.

As they do so, draw in a coloured arrow, from the subject of the sentence to the related name: so from the above suggestions there would be an arrow from John to Fay and from Jack to Tom. There will sometimes be parallel arrows; for example, a parallel arrow going the other way will be produced by the sentence:

Fay is John's wife.

By the end, every name should be linked to at least two others.

As a follow-up, point to any of the arrows, and elicit, orally or in writing, the sentence that it represents.

Variations: Put the students into pairs, and give one of them a family-tree diagram, the other a blank sheet of paper. The one with the diagram dictates the names and relationships, improvising sentences from the diagram using the possessive *'s* as above, so that the other can reconstruct it. Alternatively, each student dictates to his or her partner his or her own immediate family.

In another version, one student is given a blank diagram – just the lines, with no names – and the other a list of names and information ('Jack is Fay's son').

BOX 62

Family trees

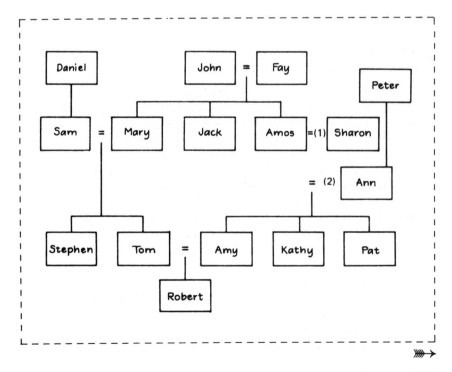

BOX 62   continued

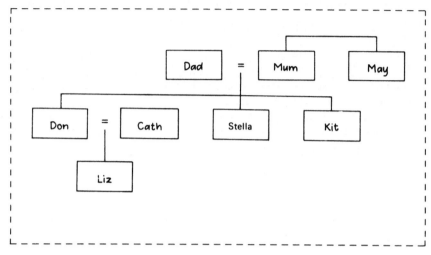

© Cambridge University Press 1988

24.3   Whose is it?

Use of 's or possessive pronouns or adjectives to indicate possession; writing; simple oral utterances based on object cues.

Materials: One or two small objects from each member of the class; each object should be in some way identifiable as belonging to its owner: a hair slide from someone with long hair, a sheet of music from someone who plays an instrument. Ask students the day before the lesson to bring the articles with them to class.

Procedure: Place the articles on a table in the middle of the room, and make sure that all the students know what they are called in English – if necessary, write up new words on the board. Then each student takes an article and notes down in writing whose he or she thinks it is:

> The hair slide is Tali's.

Then he or she returns the article and takes another, and so on, until most students have written ten or so sentences. If they aren't sure, they should guess anyway.

Check answers, using and eliciting possessive pronouns:

> Is this yours, Tali?
> No, it isn't mine. It's Anat's.

Who got the most right answers?

24.4 Distributing goods

Plural possessive pronouns and adjectives (*our, their, ours, theirs*); as a variation, other possessives; simple oral utterances based on picture cues.

Materials: Piles of pictures of objects; those in *Box 5*, page 56, can be used, or pictures cut out of magazines.

Procedure: Tell the class that the objects are available for use on a holiday: 'we' are going on an active outdoor holiday, whereas 'they' (a rival class or school) are going on a restful, luxurious one. In groups, they have to distribute the objects:

> Is this our camera or theirs?
> This is ours.

and put them into two piles according to their category.

If each group has the same set of pictures, then results can later be compared.

Variations: The same can be done with other possessives: if two holiday-makers have names, then the *'s* is used; if one is male and one is female (unnamed), then *his/her/his/hers*; if students are working in pairs, then each can take one of the roles, using *my/your/mine/yours*.

See also:
(for possessive adjectives and pronouns)
29.1 *Reverse guessing*;
29.2 *Eavesdropping*.

25 Prepositions

25.1 Finding twins (1)

Simple prepositional phrases of time and place, and their order (place before time); manipulation of set formula; oral.

Materials: Individual copies of three-by-three grids, showing alternative versions of a sentence that includes definitions of time and place: examples in *Box 63*.

Procedure: Each student marks the particular alternatives he or she prefers, and tries to find other students with the same choices, by asking simple questions based on the text of the grid:

Are you going to be in town?
Are you going to be in town at six o'clock?
Are you going to be in town on Saturday?

25.2 Finding twins (2)

Use of simple prepositions of place to describe a scene; short oral responses to picture.

Materials: Sets of pictures as in *Box 49*, page 169: about 30 pictures, which all look similar, but each picture has only one exact 'pair'. Most of the differences should be differences of position, e.g. the apple is *on* the table or *in* the tree. For instructions how to make such pictures, see 16.4 *Find a twin picture*, page 168.

Procedure: Each student gets one card, which may not be displayed to anyone else, and tries to find its 'twin' by going round and talking to other students, describing or asking questions about the content of the cards. The kinds of sentences used in these transactions may of course be prescribed in advance:

A: Where is your cat?
B: My cat is under the table.

or, more simply:

A: The bird?
B: In the tree.

If you have enough pictures, the first students to find 'twins' may be

BOX 63

Preposition grids

I am going to be ...

in town	at midnight	on Saturday
near here	in the afternoon	on May 1st
in the country	at six o'clock	on Tuesday

I spent a day ...

in London	on a Monday	in 1985
at the sea	on a Thursday	in 1987
in Scotland	on August 20th	in 1986

issued with new ones, until they run out. Then students who have finished help those who have not.

25.3 Guessing locations

Prepositions of place in 'yes/no' questions; oral interaction.

Procedure: Tell the students you have hidden an imaginary treasure somewhere in the classroom, and invite them to guess where:
> Near the window?
> Behind the blackboard?

Tell them when they are getting 'warmer' or 'colder'. Then let one of them choose where the next 'treasure' is to be located.

Variations: The 'treasure' may be located outside the classroom;

wherever you like, in fact. The more detailed the location (e.g. 'under a book on the shelf by the window in the library') the more lengthy the guessing process will be, and the more prepositional phrases will be used.

To make it more realistic you could actually secrete a (symbolic) item in the locations you choose – but I find that this is usually more trouble than it is worth; and younger classes often cannot resist the temptation to get up and look instead of asking!

25.4 Describe and arrange

Prepositions of place in instructions; oral interaction.

BOX 64

Buildings to describe

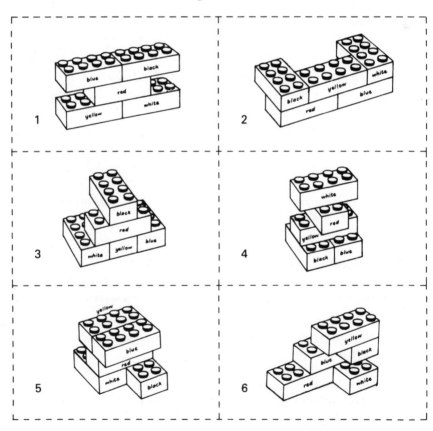

Materials: Sets of Lego blocks or Cuisenaire rods of varied sizes and colours; each student has an identical set.

Procedure: Give students instructions how to arrange the components:

Put the yellow rod across the black rod ...

Put the red brick behind the white brick ...

Then in pairs: one student arranges his or her materials in a pattern the other cannot see, and then gives instructions how to lay them out. At the end they check they have the same pattern.

Variations: Using only one set of materials per pair: the student giving the instructions gets a sketch of the desired layout instead of building it him or herself, and dictates from that. Examples in *Box 64*. If several copies of each sketch are made, they can be exchanged each time, until every pair of students has done as many as possible in the time.

BOX 64   continued

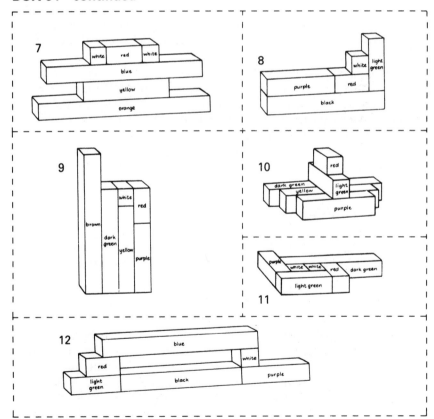

© Cambridge University Press 1988

25.5 Where would you like to live?

Use of prepositions of place or direction to locate points on a map; writing and oral interaction.

Materials: Individual copies of a fairly large-scale map of an urban or rural area; you could use the island map in *Box 55*, page 199, or the road map in *Box 33*, page 128; or a map of your own local area.

Procedure: Tell the students where you would like to live, if you could choose, in the area on the map:

> I'd like to live in the Nature Reserve, by the river, on the right bank.

Then ask each student to write down a description of where he or she would like to live; they must pinpoint the location by using at least three prepositional phrases. You might help by suggesting prepositions they could use: *near, by, on, in, under, opposite, beside, above, below, not far from, in the middle of, at the foot of, at the top of, at the end of,* etc.

They mark in on the map their chosen place to live. Then they find out where other students live, by hearing their descriptions of the location, and mark these in also.

Variations: Instead of describing the location, students can direct each other to their homes, starting, say, from the bottom left-hand corner of the map. The prepositions then will be ones of direction and movement: *to, into, past, by, along, over, under, down, up, up to, as far as, across, through, via, beyond,* etc.

Discuss: who lives near whom? What kinds of places do most students live in? Why did people choose to live where they do?

25.6 Can you remember?

Prepositions of time and place, and the ordering of prepositional phrases; construction of sentences round set pattern; oral and written.

Procedure: Can the students recall the exact place and time of an event in their lives? For instance, many older people can remember exactly where and when they heard that President Kennedy had been shot. Ask students to write down the event, and the exact place, hour, day and year. It can be something quite recent. Then each student in turn tells the others the time and place, and gives some kind of hint; and they try to guess what the event was. For example:

> In my home at two o'clock in the afternoon, on a Saturday in the autumn of 1973 ... something rather frightening happened to me.

This can be done in full class, or in small groups. If the latter, ask students later to tell the full class what each other's experiences were.

Variations: Having noted down the time and place, students can simply recount their experiences without asking others to guess. Or they can do the same as an essay for homework.

See also:

26 Present perfect

26.1 The news (1)

Use of present perfect to present current news; listening comprehension and writing from dictation.

Materials: A recording of an English-language news broadcast, preferably recent. Listen to it yourself in advance of the lesson and note down all examples of the present perfect.

Procedure: Play the recording to the students, and make sure they have understood the main news items, explaining new vocabulary as necessary. During a second and third listening they should try to jot down instances of present perfect forms as they hear them. Check results, and discuss content.

Variations: For homework, the students might try to write a news bulletin of local (or school) current affairs; when you have checked it, they could record it.

26.2 The news (2)

Use of present perfect (especially passive) to present current news; reading comprehension, and expansion of brief headlines into full sentences, in writing.

Materials: A pile of English-language newspapers.

Procedure: Ask the students to look through the headlines and first sentence or two of the news reports. They should underline – or highlight with fluorescent pens – headlines which they think imply a present perfect (they may need help with understanding some of the vocabulary). For example:

> Chairman told to quit.

They should then expand these into full present perfect sentences (often the first line or two of the article itself will show them how this should be done):

> The chairman of Brown & Smith Ltd has been told to resign.

Later, hear and discuss their examples, or take in for checking.

Comment: You may need to teach a little 'journalese' (for example, the use of short words like *quit* in headlines for the more usual *resign*), or at least explain such usages when they come up. The expansion of headlines may therefore entail some corresponding changes of vocabulary, from 'journalese' into 'normal' English. Also note that headlines in the present perfect are often explained by sentences in the past simple in the following detailed report, as the writer details times and places; this is perhaps worth pointing out to your students – a good opportunity to illustrate the difference in meaning between the two aspects.

26.3   Find someone who ...

Use of present perfect with *ever* and *never*; questions and answers based on set cues; reading and oral interaction.

Materials: A set of cards or slips of paper, each of which has a task on it beginning: 'Find someone who ', plus the present perfect. For example:
Find someone who has been to Disneyland.
Find someone who has had a car accident.
There should be about ten different tasks, each one duplicated three or four times. Examples in *Box 65*.

Procedure: Describe a task similar to those on the cards:
Find someone who has ridden an elephant.
and ask round the class:
Have you ever ridden ... ?
until you find someone who has, or until it is apparent that nobody has. Write up on the board:
Karen has ridden an elephant.
or:
No one in the class has ever ridden an elephant.
Then tell them to take a card each, and try to find someone in the class who has done the action indicated on it, by going round asking each other questions beginning 'Have you ever ... ?' They should then note down the result in a full sentence, like the one you wrote on the board, and take a new card. How many answers can they find out and write down? This is a competition, so they are not to give away the answers to each other as they find them out!

Check the answers at the end, by asking publicly for an answer to each task:
Has anyone ever ... ?
Participants get one point for each acceptable answer. Anyone who writes for any item that nobody has ever done it, when in fact there is somebody in the class who has, loses a point.

BOX 65

Find someone who ...

1 Find someone who has had a car accident.

NAME:

2 Find some who has written a letter to a newspaper.

NAME:

3 Find someone who has read *A Tale of Two Cities*

NAME:

4 Find someone who has eaten a frog.

NAME:

5 Find someone who has slept in a cave.

NAME:

6 Find someone who has been to Disneyland.

NAME:

7 Find someone who has spoken to a famous person.

NAME:

8 Find someone who has done all their homework this term.

NAME:

9 Find someone who has spent more than a month in hospital.

NAME:

BOX 65　continued

```
10  Find someone who has driven a tractor.

    NAME:
```

© Cambridge University Press 1988

26.4　What has/hasn't happened

Use of present perfect to describe what has led up to present situation; also, present perfect with *not yet*; oral brainstorm.

Materials:　Two pictures showing a situation before and after changes (*Box 55*, page 199).

Procedure:　Ask students to brainstorm what they think *has not yet happened* in the first picture, relative to the second; or what *has now happened* in the second. The same may be done in writing.

Variations:　Use only one picture, showing a more or less dramatic situation, as in *Box 28*, page 106. Students describe what *has happened* to produce the situation depicted. Then ask them to continue with what they think **may** happen, but *has not yet happened*. Again, the same may be done in writing.

26.5　Oh!

Use of present perfect to describe past events leading up to present situation; construction of simple sentences based on brief verbal cues; oral or written.

Procedure:　Give the students a series of exclamations ('Oh!', 'Ah!', 'Great!', etc. – more examples in *Box 66*), and ask them what they think has just happened to make the speaker say them. For example, 'Oh!' might mean that:

　　She has had a surprise.

or:

　　He has just remembered something.

They might brainstorm their ideas orally, or write them down. If possible, record the exclamations, or say them, rather than giving them in writing; this gives the extra dimension of intonation, and makes the meaning clearer.

Comment: Note that the material on which this activity is based is very culture-linked; similar exclamations may occur in the students' native language, with totally different meanings. You can make the English meanings clear by the use of intonation and facial expression; or you may have to explain some of them verbally.

BOX 66

Exclamations

1 Oh!	11 Great!	21 Thank you!
2 Ah!	12 Well?	22 No, thank you!
3 Oh good!	13 Sorry!	23 Rubbish!
4 Damn!	14 No!	24 Thank goodness!
5 What on earth?!	15 Yes!	25 Touch wood!
6 My God!	16 Yes?	26 Good luck!
7 Oh dear!	17 Hallo!	27 Bad luck!
8 What?	18 Hallo?	28 Congratulations!
9 Stop it!	19 (sigh)	29 Cheers!
10 Ow!	20 Welcome!	30 Goodbye!

© Cambridge University Press 1988

26.6   Accounting for moods

Use of present perfect to describe events leading up to present situation; oral or written brainstorm, based on given sentence pattern.

Materials: A set of pictures showing people in different moods: individual copies, or one set large enough to be displayed to the full class (*Box 67*).

Procedure: Go through the pictures with the students defining with them the apparent feelings of the person depicted ('worried ... surprised ... exhausted') – you may have several possibilities for each picture. Then take one picture, and ask them what they think *has happened* to make the person feel this way.

> She is worried because her young son has not come home yet, and it's very late.

Write up a few suggestions on the board. Then let them do the same in writing for other pictures, working individually or in pairs. They do not need to take the pictures in any rigid order: let them choose whichever ones they want, and do as many as they can in the time. Then hear and discuss results.

Variations: The same may be done in writing for homework.

BOX 67

Moods

BOX 67   continued

26.7 Things have changed since then

Use of present perfect to define happenings or processes during a period up to the present; oral brainstorm.

Procedure: Describe to the students some of the impressive things that have happened in the world in your lifetime:

Man has landed on the moon.

English has become the most important international language.

Ask the students if they can think of things that have happened or changed within their own memories. Help them by suggesting fields of activity: what has changed in ... fashion? means of transport? eating habits? the arts? the political scene? sport? science and technology? After finding a few examples together, as a full class, they may continue in groups, pooling and discussing results later.

Variations: Suggest that students talk in the same way about changes that have taken place in their own lives, say in the last ten years:

I have been to China.

I have learnt how to swim.

26.8 I have lived here for ...

Use of present perfect or present perfect progressive to describe a past state or process extending into the present, with *since* or *for*; writing and oral interaction.

Procedure: Ask each student to write in their notebook four to six (true) facts about themselves in the present tense; for example:

I am married.

I live here in England.

I am feeling tired.

Write on the board one or two such facts about yourself, and add present perfect sentences showing *how long* these facts have been so:

I have been married for ten years.

Then give out slips of paper, and tell students to write on each slip one such present perfect (or present perfect progressive) sentence for each of their own sentences.

I have lived here for a year.

I have been feeling tired since I got up this morning.

Take in the slips of paper, and put them in a pile on your desk.

Tell the students to choose one slip of paper each and guess who wrote it – if they have no idea, they should make a random guess anyway; and write down what they think:

Elke has been married for six years.

Jehan has always been blonde.

Then they put back the slip they have just read, and take another – until most of them have looked at and guessed the authors of about ten to 15 slips. Finally, go through the slips eliciting the correct answers; how many did they get right? Who got most right answers?

26.9 The right experience for the job

Use of present perfect to express past events with relevance for present situation; optionally, use of modal phrases *should have*, *need not have*; reading and free discussion.

Materials: Individual copies of the *curricula vitae* of four candidates for a job, showing their past experience – things they *have done* (examples in *Box 68*).

Procedure: Give the students the texts, and tell them that the people described are candidates for a specific job – teacher in this school, for example (some more suggestions at the bottom of *Box 68*). Go through the texts, if necessary, explaining any difficult vocabulary. Students then discuss who they would choose for the job on the basis of relevant past experience and their own judgement; this can be done either in full class or in small groups.

Variations: Divide the class into small groups, and ask each one to draw up what kinds of experience they think the successful candidate *must/should have had*, or *need not have had*. They then judge the candidates on the basis of their recommendations.

In another variation, only one group does the above; each of the others prepares a *curriculum vitae* for 'their' candidate, stating past experience, in a form similar to that shown in *Box 68*. The group which has drawn up the recommendations then hears the qualifications of the different candidates and chooses one. This may be done through role-play; one representative from each group is the 'candidate', and is interviewed by the selection committee.

BOX 68

Candidates for a job

JOCK, aged 30
B.A. in social studies.
Has spent a year working his way round the world.
Has spent six years teaching economics in state school.
Has written a highly successful novel about teachers.
Has lived in a back-to-nature commune for two years.
Has been married twice – now divorced. Two children.
Has been running local youth group for three years.

BETTY, aged 45
Has been married for 24 years, three children.
Has not worked most of that time.
Has done evening courses in youth guidance.
Has spent the last year teaching pupils privately for state exams – with good results.
Has been constantly active in local government – has been elected to local council twice.

ROBERT, aged 27
Has never been married, no children.
Has served a term in prison – killed a man in a drunken fight; but has committed no further crimes since release two years ago.
Has recently become a Catholic, regularly goes to church.
Has been working in school for mentally retarded in poor area – has been recommended by principal of the school.
Has followed no course of formal study.

CLAIRE, aged 60
Has been married, husband now dead, no children.
Has been a teacher for 35 years, mostly teaching English abroad.
Has lived many years in the Far East (husband was diplomat).
Has taught English in British Council school in Singapore and Hong Kong.
Has been Principal of British School for girls in Kuala Lumpur.
Husband died two years ago; since then has been in this country, doing voluntary youth work; has recently completed Diploma in Youth Counselling.

© Cambridge University Press 1988

POSSIBLE JOBS
'Buddy' (companion) for AIDS victim
Probation officer (training provided)
Children's nurse in orphanage
Teacher in special school for disturbed teenagers

27 Present progressive

27.1 Remembering pairs

('Pelmanism', 'Memory game'.) Brief present progressive sentences with subject pronouns; oral responses to picture cues.

Materials: Sets of small cards made up of matched pairs of identical pictures. Each pair depicts a person or animal doing some easily identified action: a man/woman/dog running, for example, or a girl/boy/cat eating. There should be at least 20 pairs. *Box 69* shows 30 such pictures, which you will need to copy twice to get the pairs; or you can make cards from published materials (see BIBLIOGRAPHY).

Procedure: Students work in small groups of not more than four participants. Each group has a set of cards, which are randomly distributed before them, face down. The first participant turns over any two cards and describes the pictures revealed in brief present progressive sentences:

> He is running.
> She is eating.
> They are fighting.

then replaces them face down. This process is repeated, in turn, by the participants, the aim being to remember where the different cards were

BOX 69

Action pictures for 'Remembering pairs'

located and to turn up a matching pair – which then becomes the property of the one who found them. The winner is the one who has the most pairs at the end.

BOX 69   continued

27.2 What's going on?

Use of present progressive to describe action-in-progress; oral or written brainstorm based on picture cue.

Materials: A picture showing a large number of things going on – a street scene, for example, or a family living-room. You can use the examples shown in *Box 57*, page 210, or published materials (see BIBLIOGRAPHY); or you may find suitable pictures in your coursebook. In any case, the things shown in the picture should be within the scope of the students' vocabulary. The picture should be large enough to display to the entire class – or each student may be given a copy.

Procedure: Ask students to brainstorm all the things that they can see going on in the picture:

> The policeman is talking to the driver.
> The woman is drinking coffee.

This can be done orally; or in writing, sharing results later. Can they find 20 things to say? How many activities can they identify in two minutes?

Variations: Show the picture for a minute or so, then hide it and ask students to write down all the things that they can remember are going on. Check against the picture. The same can be done as a group competition: which group has remembered the most activities?

27.3 Guessing mimes

Use of present progressive to describe action-in-progress; reading and oral guessing.

Materials: Simple sentences for guessing, using the present progressive:

> You are opening a tin.
> You are making a cup of tea.
> You are watching a comedy on television.

More examples in *Box 70*.

Alternatively, similar situations depicted in drawings.

Procedure: One student is given a cue-card, and mimes its content for the rest of the class to guess:

> Are you holding something?
> Are you opening something?

Comment: It is important in such activities to make sure that not too much time is spent only on silent mime. The students should be encouraged to keep guessing during the mime.

BOX 70

Mimes

1 You are opening a tin.

2 You are making a cup of tea.

3 You are watching a comedy on television.

4 You are trying to catch a mosquito.

5 You are reading a very sad story.

6 You are crossing a busy road.

7 You are acting in a Shakespeare play.

8 You are waiting for the dentist.

9 You are eating a very hot curry.

10 You are changing a baby's nappy.

© Cambridge University Press 1988

27.4 What does it sound like?

Use of present progressive to describe action-in-progress; oral brain-storm based on sound cues.

Materials: A recording of a series of sounds (footsteps, running water, a door slamming, and so on). You can make this yourself at home, or use published materials (see BIBLIOGRAPHY).

Procedure: Play the sequence of sounds to the students, and ask them what sort of things they think are going on. Get some suggestions:

A man is running across the room.

Someone is washing their hands.

Then replay the sequence, bit by bit this time; stop after every few seconds, and ask the students to write down what they think is happening; help with vocabulary as needed. At the end, they should get together in pairs or groups to see if they have a coherent series of events that explain the sequence of sounds – all in the present progressive, of course. Then hear and compare the different versions.

Variations: Use a sequence of different pieces of music in contrasting moods, instead of sound effects. Tell the students that the music is the background to a brief video sequence; can they reconstruct what is going on? Otherwise the procedure is as above. This is more demanding of their imaginations, but results in more varied and interesting stories.

27.5 Silhouettes

Use of the present progressive to describe action-in-progress, mainly in the interrogative; oral brainstorming.

Materials: A series of silhouettes showing people in the process of some action, usually holding, or standing by, some object or instrument. These may be made easily by sticking magazine pictures of suitable figures on black paper, then cutting out. The resulting silhouette may then be displayed against a background of white paper, or a whiteboard, if you have one; or simply laid on the overhead projector. Some examples in *Box 71a*; solutions in *Box 71b*.

Procedure: Present the first silhouette and invite students to guess what sort of a person it is and what he or she is doing.

Is he holding something?

Is he holding a musical instrument?

They may need some new vocabulary; supply as needed.

Variations: You can put up several silhouettes at once, numbering them, and ask students to guess whichever one they like. This means that when they despair of, or get fed up with, one of them they can move on to one of the others. This tends to speed up the rate of suggestions, and therefore increase the amount of practice.

BOX 71a

Silhouettes

© Cambridge University Press 1988

Activities

BOX 71b

Silhouettes (solutions)

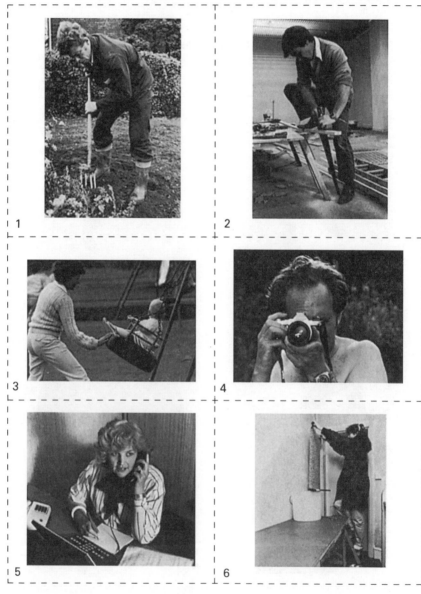

27.6 Temporary and permanent

Use of the present progressive to indicate a temporary state or action; contrast with present simple; composition of sentences based on set formula; written and oral.

Procedure: Describe to the class some things you are doing temporarily, and contrast with more permanent or usual situations:

> At the moment I'm speaking English, but most of the time I speak French.
>
> This year I'm living in Paris, but my permanent home is in Scotland.

Ask the students to write down a few similar sentences. They may begin them with:

> At the moment ...
>
> Today ...
>
> These days ...
>
> This year/month/week ...

and they may choose as their subject someone well known to them – it does not have to be themselves. They then read out their sentences to each other, in the full class or in small groups. Encourage them to ask each other questions:

> Are you enjoying living in Paris?
>
> Where do you live in Scotland?

Variations: Tell students to read out only one half of their sentence:

> At the moment I'm not feeling very well ...

and ask others to try to reconstruct what the other half is. The one who guesses nearest the original suggests the next half-sentence.

See also:

28 Present simple

28.1 Opinion polls

Use of present simple to describe states of feeling, thinking, etc.; reading and answering set questions; optional free discussion or writing as follow-up.

Materials: Individual copies of questionnaires designed to elicit opinions on some subject of interest to the class. My example (*Box 72*) is a feedback sheet on the English course the students are currently doing; but you could construct similar questionnaires on any topic of general or local interest (see *Box 43c*, page 156). Or use questionnaires like those in *Boxes 40, 43a* and *43b*, pages 144, 153 and 154.

Procedure: Give out the questionnaires, and go through them if necessary checking that they are understood. Ask students to read the questions and tick their answers. Or they can administer the questionnaires to each other, marking down their partner's responses. They may then compare and talk about their answers.

Variations: For homework, each student writes a summary of his or her opinion of the topic of the questionnaire, in essay form, using the questionnaire answers as a source of ideas.

They may also be asked to design their own questionnaires, eliciting opinions of classmates on topics that interest them (some possible topics in *Box 43c*, page 156).

BOX 72

Feedback on this course

Please tick the appropriate answer.

> 1 How much do you feel you have learnt on this course so far?
> A lot / quite a lot / not much / nothing

BOX 72 continued

2 Do you find the material: too easy?
                               too difficult?
                               about the right level of difficulty?

3 How do you rate the teaching?
Excellent / good / all right / not very good / bad / terrible

4 Do you think you get: too much homework?
                            too little homework?
                            about the right amount of homework?

5 Do you consider the material interesting?
Yes, very / yes, quite / no, not very / no, it's very boring

6 Do you want: more grammar?
                more vocabulary work?
                more listening?
                more talking?
                more reading?
                more writing?

7 In general, do you prefer: working on your own?
                                 working in small groups?
                                 working in the full class,
                                      teacher-directed?

8 Do you think you should have tests: once a week?
                                      once a month?
                                      less than once a month?
                                      never?

9 Do you like playing games in class?
Yes / sometimes / no

10 Do you enjoy being with the other students, as friends?
Yes, very much / yes / no, not particularly / no, not at all

If you have any further comments, please write them below.

28.2 Animal habits

Use of present simple to describe habitual action; composition of simple sentences; oral or written.

Procedure: Give the class the name of an animal, and ask them what they know about its habits. For example, a rabbit:

> It lives in a hole.
> It eats plants and vegetables.
> It has a lot of babies.
> It runs very fast.

If they get stuck, suggest verbs they might base their sentences on (*live, eat, move, mate, sleep, make, change, grow, die, give birth*), rather than limiting them with non-open-ended questions like 'Where does it live?'

Then ask them, in groups or pairs, to prepare a description of the habits of an animal of their choice. Each group later reads out its description to the rest of the class, who guess what the animal is.

Variations: For homework, ask the students to choose an animal and find out as much as they can about it, by looking it up in nature or zoology books, encyclopaedias and so on (if these are in English so much the better, but such material can also be read in the native language). Then they should write a brief essay in English about their animal.

In a later lesson, invite them to give brief talks about the animals they have studied.

28.3 Routines

Use of the present simple to describe routine actions; composition of sentences based on time expressions; oral and written.

Procedure: Discuss briefly activities we do as part of our daily routine; and ask for examples of things people do regularly once a week, once a month, once a year.

> I visit my grandmother once a month.
> I take my vitamin pill once a day.

Then give the students five minutes to write down as many things as they can think of that they do:

1 Every day
2 About once a month
3 About once a year

They should write their suggestions in full sentences, like the examples above; supply new vocabulary as needed.

In groups, they read out their lists to one another, and delete anything they have written down which someone else has as well. So that at the end, each student has only his or her 'special' routines, that no one else has. Later, a representative from each group describes these 'special' routines in the third person:

Justine goes to ballet class every day.

Paul doesn't eat anything for one day every month.

Some of these routines may give rise to interesting questions and answers – also in the present simple.

28.4   What's my line?

Use of present simple to describe habitual action, mostly interrogative; contrast between present simple and present progressive; oral guessing.

Materials: Slips of paper, on each of which is written the name of a profession (examples in *Box 73*).

Procedure: One student takes a slip, and does a mime showing some activity which a person would do in the course of the job indicated – but not something which immediately gives it away. For example, a 'bus-driver' could mime locking up the bus, rather than steering and changing gear!

Other students try to guess what the job is; they may ask general questions, in the present simple:

Do you work outside?

or questions connected with the mime, in the present progressive:

In your mime, are you holding something?

They may only make three direct guesses as to the profession ('Are you a secretary?'), so should be very sure of their ground before doing so.

BOX 73

Professions

1 policeman/woman	6 actor/actress	11 secretary
2 teacher	7 farmer	12 bus-driver
3 mechanic	8 hairdresser	13 pilot
4 photographer	9 model	14 singer
5 road-cleaner	10 chef	15 computer programmer

28.5 What I do

Use of present simple to describe habitual action or state; writing and free discussion.

Materials: Individual copies of forms showing various fields of activity (sport, eating, hobbies, entertainment, etc.), with room to write in full sentences (*Box 74*).

Procedure: Ask students to write in one sentence stating one thing they do – or don't do – in each field. For example:

    SPORT: I watch tennis, but I don't play it.

    EATING: I don't eat pork, as I am Jewish.

    HOBBIES: I collect matchboxes.

Then students get into pairs and tell each other about themselves. Finally, each student tells the rest of the class about his or her partner:

    Yossi watches tennis, but doesn't play it ... he doesn't eat pork because he is Jewish ... he collects matchboxes...

Comment: This is a good activity for the beginning of the course, when students are still getting to know one another.

BOX 74

Things I do

WORK	
HOBBIES	
SPORT	

BOX 74 continued

EATING	
ENTERTAINMENT	
SOCIAL	
CLOTHES	
HOUSEWORK	
FAMILY	
TRAVEL	

28.6 Something special

Use of present simple to describe habitual action or state; oral inter-action, and/or writing.

Procedure: Ask each student to write down one interesting (present) fact about him or herself (an unusual hobby, habit, job, possession, ability, disability) that he or she would be willing to talk about:

I go bird-watching every weekend.

I only eat natural foods.

– and do the same yourself. Then you and individual students present your topics, talk about them briefly, and answer questions.

Variations: Students can write about their topics instead of discussing them; or write as a preparation for oral presentation and discussion.

Comment: Again, a good getting-to-know-you activity.

28.7 Associations

Use of present simple to describe feeling, opinion, etc.; free composition of sentences based on picture cues; oral.

Materials: A pile of smallish pictures depicting objects, animals, scenes. You can use simple drawings, like those in *Box 5*, page 56; but colour photographs cut out of magazines are better.

Procedure: Spread the pictures on a table in the middle of the class-room, and invite each student to choose one that arouses some kind of definite positive or negative reaction in him or her. Then invite each to show his or her picture and say whether he or she likes it or not, and why. Start the ball rolling yourself:

I like this picture of a dog – I love dogs, and this one reminds me of our own dog at home.

Comment: Not all the student responses will be in the present simple; they may respond to a picture because it reminds them of something that happened in the past, or something they hope will happen in the future. This is perfectly acceptable; the main thing is that the students' descriptions of their own reactions ('I think/feel/like/hate . . .') should be in the present simple.

28.8 Things in common

Use of present simple to describe habitual action or state; free oral interaction and writing.

Procedure: Put students in pairs, tell them to talk to each other and try to find as many things as they can in common with one another in three minutes. These should **not** include things they can find out just by looking at one another, e.g. that they both have blue eyes or are wearing jeans; nor should they include more than two things beginning 'We both like . . .'

They should write down the things they find out they have in common in full sentences:

We both have two brothers.

We both like reading detective stories.

Then ask the pairs to describe their common features. Which pair found most?

Variations: Each student has to find at least one thing in common with as many other members of the class as they can; each talks to a partner for as long as necessary to discover a common feature, then changes partners. They note down names and common features as they find them. At the end, call out pairs of names at random, and find out what they have in common.

Comment: Another good getting-to-know-you activity.

28.9 Proverbs

Use of present simple to express general truths or make generalizations; reading and free discussion.

Materials: Individual copies of a list of well-known proverbs using the present simple. There is a selection in *Box 75*; you can find more in books of proverbs (see BIBLIOGRAPHY, under *Other sources*).

Procedure: Read through the list of proverbs with the class, clarifying any difficult vocabulary and making sure the significance of each is understood. Then divide the class into small groups, and ask each group to pick out proverbs they think are untrue or misleading, discuss what is wrong with them, and invent a version that seems to them preferable. At the end, come together and discuss each proverb and its new versions.

Variations: Students can be asked to learn the proverbs by heart; then ask them to recall and write out as many as they can.

It is quite interesting to compare parallel proverbs in the students' native language, and discuss differences/similarities.

BOX 75

Proverbs in the present simple

1 A rolling stone gathers no moss.
2 Still waters run deep.
3 Eavesdroppers hear no good of themselves.
4 Love makes the world go round.
5 Actions speak louder than words.
6 Too many cooks spoil the broth.
7 A bad workman blames his tools.
8 Every cloud has a silver lining.
9 Absence makes the heart grow fonder.
10 The early bird catches the worm.
11 A new broom sweeps clean.
12 Dreams go by contraries.
13 It's an ill wind that blows nobody any good.
14 Familiarity breeds contempt.
15 Bad news travels fast.
16 The more you have the more you want.
17 Nothing succeeds like success.
18 God helps them that help themselves.
19 Practice makes perfect.
20 Two wrongs don't make a right.

© Cambridge University Press 1988

28.10 Theme music

Use of present simple to recount the plot of a book, film, etc.; free writing.

Procedure: Play the class a recording of music, chosen according to your own taste, and tell them this is the theme music of a film. Can they imagine what kind of film it is, and what sort of plot it has? They need not write down an entire story, but should note down some details of a plot that seems to them to fit the music:

> This must be a romantic film ... it's about a girl who falls in love with a handsome nobleman ... but he already has a wife ... in the end they all die ...

28.11 Recall the plot

Use of present simple to recount the plot of a story, play, film, etc.; free discussion and writing.

Procedure: Tell the students about a film you have seen or a book you have read recently: recount the plot briefly, in the present simple. Get one or two of the students to do the same. Then ask students to write an essay recommending to you a film or book that they have found particularly good; the essay should include a resumé of the plot.

Variations: Have a 'May I recommend?' session in class: students recommend to one another films, books, or plays, recounting parts of their plots. They may improvise their recommendations orally, or read out the essays they have written.

See also:
2.3   *Frequency surveys;*
2.4   *What do you do when . ...?;*
4.2   *Similarities;*
5.8   *Preferences;*
7.1   *Defining by sense;*
7.2   *Not what it seems;*
14.2 *Opinion questionnaire;*
15.5 *Common denominator;*
27.6 *Temporary and permanent;*
30.2 *Clues for solving.*

29 Pronouns

29.1 Reverse guessing

Subject and object pronouns, and possibly possessive adjectives, in simple sentences; oral brainstorm.

Procedure: One student is sent out of the room, and the rest of the class choose an object or person to be guessed. When the student comes back, he or she is told if the item to be guessed is masculine, feminine or neuter gender, and whether it is singular or plural. The 'knowers' then throw out hint after hint as to what the item is, using the appropriate pronouns, until the student is enabled to guess the answer. For example, if the answer is 'a (female) hairdresser', the class may say things like:

> She uses scissors.
> She works inside.
> She needs special training.

The guesser should be instructed not to guess, even if he or she is fairly sure of the answer, until the rest of the class have exhausted their ideas for hints.

For a written assignment to follow, students can be asked to compose a series of hints in the form of simple sentences intended to lead to a certain solution. If this is done for homework, you then have not only to correct the grammar of the sentences, but also to guess the solutions. If done in class, the sets of sentences can be exchanged between students for guessing.

29.2 Eavesdropping

Various kinds of pronouns and possessive adjectives in dialogue; reading, interpreting and adding to set texts, orally or in writing.

Materials: Short dialogues, using a lot of pronouns and possessive adjectives, but with no antecedents, so the context is unclear. Some examples in *Box 76*; see also BIBLIOGRAPHY.

Procedure: Tell the students they are eavesdropping on a dialogue – but they missed the beginning of it, so they don't know who the people are

265

that are being talked about, or what the circumstances are. Can they suggest an interpretation? Work together with them on one dialogue, gathering various suggestions, then put them into pairs to work on another. Having decided on their interpretations, each pair of students then composes a beginning to their dialogue, which supplies antecedents to the pronouns, and explains what is being talked about.

Variations: The pairs decide how they understand their dialogues and then act them, without any additions, to the rest of the class, trying to make their interpretation as clear as possible through intonation, gesture, etc. If the rest of the class cannot guess, they then explain who they think is being talked about and why.

Or students can compose their own similar dialogues, whose explanations only they know, for others to work out.

Comment: This activity covers a wider range of pronominal forms than the previous one, and provides opportunities for you to review some commonly confused forms (*themselves*, not *theirself*, for example), pronominal expressions (like *by himself*) or the differences between, say, *her* and *hers*.

See also:
15.6 *Guessing*;
24.3 *Whose is it?*;
24.4 *Distributing goods.*

BOX 76

Pronoun dialogues

Dialogue 1

A: ... I told her there'd be no trouble, but she wouldn't listen.
B: They never do, none of them. But she's the worst of them all.
A: What do you think he'll do when we tell him?
B: Don't know. He can't manage by himself, anyhow. He'll need our help.
A: Ours, and theirs too.

Dialogue 2

A: Whose are they?
B: How should I know? Not mine – and not hers either.
A: We found their suitcase in your apartment.They must have been there themselves.
B: This one? Are you sure it's theirs? Anyway, it's not my apartment, it's his. Why don't you ask him?

Dialogue 3

A: You really ought to tell him yourself it's yours.
B: Me? I can't. He'll kill me. Or kill himself.
A: He'll find out by himself sooner or later.
B: Not if I can keep her quiet. She's the one I'm scared of.
A: Yes, well, it's hers too in a way, isn't it?

Dialogue 4

A: Pick him up!
B: Pick him up yourself! He's yours, not mine!
A: I'm busy with her. She's the difficult one.
B: I think he's the worse of the two. He's uglier than her. I won't touch him.

30 Relative clauses

30.1 Likes and dislikes

Use of relative clauses to define nouns; composing sentences based on set pattern; writing and oral interaction.

Procedure: Give the class the introductory cues:
> I like people who ...
> I dislike people who ...

and ask everyone to complete the sentences in writing according to their own opinions and preferences. Then ask them to tell you what they have written, and write up the results on the board: you then have a profile of the class's favourite – and un-favourite – people!

Variations: Give the students similar beginnings, but with different nouns, using a variety of types of relatives: 'days when...', 'places where...', 'teachers who...', 'films which...', 'lessons in which...'

Instead of pooling the students' sentences in the full class they can do the same in groups; or each student can go round trying to find someone else with the same likes and dislikes as him or herself.

30.2 Clues for solving

Use of relative clauses to define nouns; composing noun phrases with relative clauses; mainly reading and writing.

Materials: A number of lists of different nouns, known to the students; all the nouns on any one list should begin with the same letter. Some examples in *Box 77*.

Procedure: Write up one such list on the board, and ask students to suggest definitions for each item, using relative clauses. For example:

> A POLICEMAN: Someone who directs traffic
> A POST OFFICE: A place where you can buy stamps

Divide the class into pairs or small groups, give each of these one such list and ask them to make up a similar definition for each noun. They then copy out their definitions, without the original nouns. The lists of definitions are exchanged, and students work on each other's clues: what were the original nouns? And which letter began them all? If there

are not too many, read out the clues and check answers at the end.
Variations: You may ask the students themselves to compose the
original list of nouns, instead of giving it to them ready-made.

BOX 77

Nouns for defining

List 1	*List 2*	*List 3*
a policeman	a duck	a book
a parrot	a doctor	Bangladesh
a pen	Denmark	bread
a pear	a door	a bedroom
Poland	December	a baby
a post office	a dream	a bottle
a panda	a daughter	a bus
pre-history	a dollar	a birthday

List 4	*List 5*	*List 6*
Australia	Hollywood	spaghetti
an apple	a helicopter	a shoe
August	a hand	Saudi Arabia
an airport	a hotel	a shop
an artist	a holiday	a snake
an African	a hairdresser	the sun
an alligator	history	the summer
acid	a horse	a scientist

List 7	*List 8*	*List 9*
a cow	a television	the morning
Canada	Thailand	Malaysia
a chicken	a tomato	a mother
a carpenter	a tiger	a motorbike
a cigarette	tennis	a map
coffee	a taxi-driver	matches
a cinema	a ticket	money
Christmas	a tooth	milk

>>>→

BOX 77 continued

List 10	*List 11*	*List 12*
night	wine	an egg
New Zealand	Wales	England
a newspaper	the winter	an elephant
a nurse	a wife	the evening
a nut	a witch	an emperor
a neighbour	a water	an engine
a nose	the west	economics
a name	a wall	an entrance

© Cambridge University Press 1988

Comment: You might prefer to spread this activity over two sessions; this gives you time to take in the lists of definitions and check and correct them before giving them out to be guessed.

During the second (guessing) stage it is a good idea to tell students to write their solutions on a separate piece of paper; then the list of clues can be passed on to other students for guessing.

30.3 Write your own test

Use of relative clauses for defining nouns; composition of relative clauses based on noun cues.

Materials: A list of nouns, or noun phrases, and adjectives that the class has learnt recently.

Procedure: This is really a variation of 30.2 *Clues for solving*, but rather more serious and challenging. Tell the students they are going to write their own vocabulary tests, which will be administered next lesson. Give them the list of vocabulary, and ask each student, or each pair of students, to write a definition of ten of the items, using relative clauses. Beside each definition they leave a dotted line where the answer will be filled in.

A woman whose main job is looking after the home: ....
With adjectives, they write a definition of a noun described by the adjective, and then put the noun beside the dotted line. For example:

A man who has never learnt very much : An .... man.
They then exchange and do each other's tests.

Variations: You can take in their papers after the first session for checking and correcting, then administer the tests next time.

If you have time, you might like to type out and make multiple copies of the tests for administering later. In any case, the solutions are best checked orally, in the full class.

Comment: An excellent way to consolidate vocabulary!

30.4 Elaborating a story

Use of non-defining relative clauses for description; free composition of clauses based on noun cues; oral or written.

Materials: Any short story or anecdote, taken from your coursebook or from published collections of stories (see BIBLIOGRAPHY). Copy out the story, leaving a comma and half-line gap after some of the nouns. For example:
Once upon a time, there was a girl called Goldilocks, ...
.... She lived in a house, ...,
with her mother, ...

Procedure: Give each student a copy of the story, and ask them, in pairs, to invent and write in relative clauses. These can be conventional and appropriate to the story:
Goldilocks, who was very pretty and had long golden hair.
or you can ask for original and unexpected ones:
Goldilocks, whose hair was really brown (but she dyed it yellow).
At the end, hear suggestions and choose one for each space; finally, read out the finished story.

Variations: Don't tell the students what the story is, but just give them each noun in turn, out of context, and ask for suggestions for a relative clause describing it. Fill in the most incongruous or original suggestion each time; when all the nouns have been described, read out the result, or show it on the overhead projector: it can be very entertaining.

30.5 Let's complain

Relative clauses with prepositions; brainstorming noun phrases with relative clauses, and constructing sentences based on them; mostly oral.

Procedure: Tell the students they (and you!) are going to have a complaining session – let off steam about all the things that bother them. But first they have to think of things to complain about; and these must be expressed by nouns with relative clauses that use prepositions. For example, they might like to complain about:

The people I work with

The house/town I live in

The book we learn from

The person I sat next to in the bus today

Get the students to brainstorm as many such phrases as they can think of, and write them on the board. You might help them by suggesting topics: people, surroundings, equipment, entertainment. Then ask them to let loose their complaints! They can, of course, add to, modify or present variations of each other's suggestions.

Variations: After the brainstorm, you might give them a few minutes to write down some complaints before sharing them orally.

As a follow-up they might discuss what they could do about the various problems. Invite students to offer each other friendly advice.

For homework, ask them to recall and write down things they and other people complained about. Or make a list of things they are **pleased** about, and write similar sentences about them.

Comment: It is up to you, of course, what exact forms you wish the relative clauses to take: you might wish to include the relative pronouns:

The book which we learn from

The person who I sat next to

Or you might wish to use more formal phrasing, putting the preposition at the beginning of the relative clause:

The people with whom I work

The house in which I live

In any case, make it clear through your own first examples what pattern(s) you wish your students to follow.

31   Short answers

31.1   Answering guesses

Short answers to 'yes/no' questions; oral.

Procedure: Divide the class into two teams, each of which chooses three
items; one person, one object, one group of things or people. They then
proceed to guess each other's items.

The first team tells the second whether the item is represented by *he*,
she, *it* or *they*. Then anyone in the second team may ask 'yes/no'
questions to elicit information, and anyone in the first team may reply –
but the responses must include 'short answers', not just 'yes' or 'no':

Yes, it is.

No, we can't.

No, they don't.

They may go on guessing and answering until all items have been
discovered (or despaired of); or you may prefer to set a time limit or a
limit on the number of questions for each item. When the first three
items have been guessed, teams may go on to set further ones.

Comment: It is a good idea to check the items teams choose before the
guessing starts, to make sure they are not too easy or difficult. Or
prepare your own items in advance to give to each team.

31.2   Don't say yes or no

Short answers to 'yes/no' questions, without using 'yes' or 'no'; oral.

Procedure: The objective is to try to get other students to say 'yes' or
'no'. Any student may address a question to any other member of the
class – but the answer must be in the form of a short answer, without
saying 'yes' or 'no'. Anyone who makes a correct short answer without
'yes' or 'no' gets one mark; anyone who makes an incorrect response or
uses 'yes' or 'no' deducts a mark. After a few such exchanges, when the
procedure and scoring system are clear, divide the class into groups and
tell them to continue similar exchanges within their groups, making
sure that all group members get equal opportunities to ask and answer.
At the end, ask for groups' total scores. Which group won?

31.3 Written enquiries

'Yes/no' questions and short answers, in writing.

Materials: A pile of small blank pieces of paper.

Procedure: Give each student the name of one other student. Then each student takes a piece of paper and writes on it a 'yes/no' question addressed to the person he or she has been allotted. It should be something which he or she is genuinely interested to know. The paper is then folded, the name of the addressee written on the outside, and passed to the addressee. The addressee writes a short answer:

> Yes, I do.
> No, they aren't.

– but may also add any extra details if he or she wishes:

> Yes, I do, sometimes. But not so much as I used to.

The note is then returned to the original asker.

As soon as any student has finished writing one question, or finished writing an answer, he or she takes another piece of paper and writes another question addressed to someone else.

At the end, ask students to read out exchanges they think are particularly interesting.

See also:

15.1 *Dialogues* (using short answers in the basic texts);

15.4 *Questionnaires* (responding orally with short answers).

32 Tag questions

32.1 It's true, isn't it?

Use of tag questions to check information, using both rising and falling intonation patterns; free composition of sentences; writing and oral interaction.

Procedure: Each student writes down some things that he or she thinks he or she remembers about other members of the class, in the form of simple statements.

> Anne lived in Argentina for three years.
> Don hates snakes.

Give them a few minutes to write sentences; then tell them to go to the people they have written about and check their information. Remind them that the tag questions should have a falling intonation if the asker is fairly sure of the answer, and a rising one if not.

> Anne, you lived in Argentina for three years, didn't you? (sure)

> Don, you hate snakes, don't you? (not sure)

They tick the facts they got right and correct the ones they got wrong.

Variations: Ask all the students to write up on the board subjects they feel they could answer questions about: special skills, hobbies, jobs, fields of knowledge. Then all the students write down things they think they know about other people's fields of expertise, and check them, as described in *Procedure* above. When answering, the 'experts' may of course add further details and information. At the end, ask students to share new things they have learnt.

32.2 We both know ...

Use of tag questions in casual chat to show expectation of agreement or common knowledge, using a mainly falling intonation; inserting tag questions into set (dialogue) texts.

Materials: Individual copies of a set of five or six short written dialogues; these can be taken from your textbook or from published collections of dialogues (see BIBLIOGRAPHY); some examples in *Box 78*.

Activities

Procedure: Put the students into pairs, and ask each pair to choose one of the dialogues and insert tag questions where they feel the speakers are expecting agreement or sympathy, or talking about something both know about. What difference do the insertions make to the implications of the dialogue? Ask pairs to perform the two versions of their dialogue, making the difference clear.

BOX 78

Dialogues for adding tags

Dialogue 1

A: Nice day.
B: It'll rain tomorrow.
A: Why should it?
B: It's the picnic tomorrow. Always rains for the picnic.
A: You are in a lousy mood today.

Dialogue 2

A: I think I'll try this one.
B: Oh, yes, a lovely colour. Just matches your eyes.
A: How much is it?
B: Twenty pounds. It's much cheaper than the red one.
A: But the red one will wash better.

Dialogue 3

A: I really don't know what to do ...
B: Well, that's why you're here. You can't keep it to yourself forever.
A: I've been such a fool.
B: No you haven't. We all make mistakes sometimes.
A: It helps, talking to someone about it.

BOX 78   continued

Dialogue 4

A: You know where the microfilm is.
B: I've told you again and again that I don't.
A: We'll just have to help you remember.
B: I can't remember what I don't know.
A: That's what we're going to find out ...

Dialogue 5

A: You know I love you.
B: Yes, but ...
A: I wouldn't ask you to do something wrong.
B: You haven't told Jean?
A: No, of course not. It'll be a secret between the two of us.

Dialogue 6

A: Very good, Georgie, that's a beautiful picture.
B: I can paint all over Pattie's picture now.
A: No, Georgie, we don't spoil other people's pictures.
B: I do.
A: Now you've made poor little Pattie cry.
B: Get lost.
A: Georgie, that's not the way we talk to our teacher ...

33 TO form of the verb

33.1 What to do

Use of *to* form of the verb after question words *who, where, when, what, whether, how*; constructing written sentences based on given pattern, followed by oral interaction.

Procedure: Divide the class into an even number of groups. Half of these groups are told that they are tourists planning to visit an island they know nothing about. The others are groups of natives of various such islands. The tourists draw up a list of things they would need to find out. Give them a list beginning:

> We would need to find out ...
>
> ... how to get to the capital.
>
> ... where to stay.

and ask them to complete it with as many other similar queries as they can think of. Meanwhile each of the other groups chooses a name for their island and then makes a list of their own, beginning:

> We can tell them ...
>
> ... how to get to the capital.
>
> ... where to stay.

– but they also, of course, have to agree on their answers. Then each tourist group joins up with a native group to ask:

> Can you tell us ... ?

and notes down the information they are given. The native group may also add:

> You didn't ask ...

and may give extra information.

If you have time, let every tourist group meet every native group, and decide in the end which island they would choose to visit.

33.2 Wants

Use of *to* form of the verb after verbs like *want* + object ('I want you to...', 'He would like me to...', 'We asked you to...'): constructing sentences based on set pattern; written.

Materials: A set of pictures of people talking to one another, as in *Box 39*, page 141 – displayed, or distributed as individual copies.

Procedure: Elicit from students suggestions as to what each character in the different picture might want from the other:

The patient wants the doctor to cure him.

The girl on the left wants the girl on the right to keep her secret.

Brainstorm as many ideas as possible for each picture. For homework, give students more pictures (possibly from your coursebook), and ask them to do the same in writing.

Variations: The same can be done with fictional characters, if you are reading literature with your class: what does each character in the story want from the others? This is a good way into a general discussion of character.

Or ask students to write down what their parents want them to do; and then divide their sentences into 'Things they want me to do, and I want too' and 'Things they want me to do, but I don't want for myself.' Good for teenagers.

Comment: My examples are based on the verb *want*; but other common verbs such as *ask, tell, would like, expect, advise, warn, persuade*, etc. can be practised through similar activities.

33.3 Purposes

Use of *to* + verb to express purpose; free composition of sentences based on cues.

Procedure: Write on the board a few names of locations: local institutions or shops, or places of interest (shown in *Box 79*), and elicit suggestions why we might go to each one:

THE BANK: We'd go there to get money.

THE CAPITAL: We'd go there to see the sights.

Then divide into groups, ask each group to make its own list of places, and suggest a similar sentence for each one. They then read out their sentences, and other groups guess what the places were.

⟫→

BOX 79

Places to visit for a purpose

1 THE BANK	8 THE CAPITAL	15 THE COUNTRY
2 THE POST OFFICE	9 A HAIRDRESSER	16 THE THEATRE
3 A SUPERMARKET	10 A CLINIC	17 A CHEMIST
4 A HOTEL	11 A BUS STOP	18 A TRAVEL AGENT
5 A SCHOOL	12 A PUB or BAR	19 A GARAGE
6 THE BEACH	13 A PARK	20 THE ZOO
7 THE RIVER	14 A GYM	21 A SWIMMING POOL

© Cambridge University Press 1988

See also:
6.5 *If only*;
13.6 *What would you need to know?*;
17.3 *Desert island equipment.*

34 Used to

34.1 How things used to be

Used to to describe past habits or states, contrasted with present; free composition of written or oral sentences.

Procedure: Ask students to brainstorm a list of manufactured products they possess or often use; suggest things connected with transport, instant food, clothes, entertainment, the media, their studies. You might get things like: a car, a tin of sardines, jeans, a newspaper and so on. Then ask the students to go back in their imaginations to the 19th century – or even to the Middle Ages – when these things did not exist, and describe what people *used to* do instead of using them. They can do this orally, or in writing, giving you their ideas later.

People used to travel by horse, or by carriage.

People used to keep food by salting it.

Women used to wear dresses all the time.

Write up their suggestions on the board, and then discuss: what were the advantages and disadvantages of the different things that *used to* be or happen?

34.2 Have I changed?

Used to to describe past habits or states, contrasted with the present; written composition, possible discussion follow-up.

Procedure: Ask students to consider how their personalities, or personal habits, have changed over the last ten years (or 20 years, for mature students). Each should write down some things they *used to* be, or enjoy, or do, and contrast them with the present:

I used to do a lot of sport – but today I only play tennis.

I used to be much more irritable than I am now.

Variations: When they have finished writing, students may simply give their compositions in to you. Or ask them to get into groups and share some of their ideas – see if they have some '*used-to*'s in common. Then report back:

Both Ilana and I used to eat a lot of sweet things – but we don't any more.

See also:

Bibliography

Grammar books

Comprehensive grammars

Quirk, R. and Greenbaum, S., *A University Grammar of English*, Longman, 1973.
Quirk, R., Greenbaum, S., Leech, G. and Svartvik, J., *A Comprehensive Grammar of the English Language*, Longman, 1975.

Shorter books of grammar and usage

Leech, G., Deuchar, M. and Hoogenraad, R., *English Grammar for Today*, Macmillan, 1983.
Swan, M., *Practical English Usage*, Oxford University Press, 1980.

Grammar practice activities

Carrier, M. and the Centre for British Teachers, *Take 5: games and activities for the language learner*, Harrap, 1983.
Frank, C. and Rinvolucri, M., *Grammar in Action*, Pergamon, 1983.
Jones, L., *Ideas*, Cambridge University Press, 1984.
Jones, L., *Use of English*, Cambridge University Press, 1985.
Klippel, F., *Keep Talking*, Cambridge University Press, 1985.
Rinvolucri, M., *Grammar Games*, Cambridge University Press, 1986.
[Also, look at journals for English teachers; especially *Modern English Teacher* (Modern English Publications) and *Practical English Teaching* (Mary Glasgow Publications).]

Dialogues

Maley, A. and Duff, A., *Variations on a theme*, Cambridge University Press, 1978.

Questionnaires

Eysenck, H. J. and Wilson, G., *Know your own Personality*, Pelican, 1976.
Porter Ladousse, G., *Speaking Personally*, Cambridge University Press, 1983.

Bibliography

Quizzes

Ridout, R., *Did you Know?*, Evans Brothers, 1975.
Ridout, R., *The Long and the Short of it*, Evans Brothers, 1975.

Recorded sounds

Maley, A. and Duff, A., *Sounds Interesting*, Cambridge University Press, 1975.
Maley, A. and Duff, A., *Sounds Intriguing*, Cambridge University Press, 1979.

Stories

Hill, L. A., *Stories for Reading Comprehension*, Books 1, 2, and 3, Longman, 1985.
Morgan, J. and Rinvolucri, M., *Once Upon a Time*, Cambridge University Press, 1983.
[Also, look at short stories in the simplified readers published by Longman, Heinemann, Evans, etc.]

Visual materials

Posters

Byrne, D., *Progressive Picture Compositions*, Longman, 1967.
Byrne, D. and Hall, D., *Wall Pictures for Language Practice*, Longman, 1976.

Small pictures for interaction

Byrne, D., *Materials for Language Teaching 1 & 2: Interaction Packages A and B*, Modern English Publications, 1978.
Wright, A., *1000 Pictures for Teachers to Copy*, Collins Educational, 1984.

Other sources for specific materials

Dreyfuss, H., *Symbol Sourcebook*, McGraw Hill Book Company, 1972.
'Trivial Pursuit', Kenner Parker Toys International.
Wilson, F. P. (ed.), *Oxford Dictionary of English Proverbs*, Oxford University Press, 1970.
Woods, E., *Superstitions*, Evans Brothers, 1976.

Index

Index